IN DEFENSE OF NATURE

IN DEFENSE OF NATURE

The Catholic Unity of
Environmental, Economic,
and Moral Ecology

BENJAMIN WIKER

EMMAUS
ROAD
PUBLISHING

Steubenville, Ohio
www.emmausroad.org

Emmaus Road Publishing
1468 Parkview Circle
Steubenville, Ohio 43952

Library of Congress Cataloging-in-Publication Data

Names: Wiker, Benjamin, 1960- author.
Title: In defense of nature : the catholic unity of environmental, economic,
  and moral ecology / Benjamin Wiker.
Description: Steubenville : Emmaus Road Pub., 2017.
Identifiers: LCCN 2017009102 | ISBN 9781945125416 (hardcover)
Subjects: LCSH: Ecotheology. | Nature--Religious aspects--Christianity. |
  Environmental ethics. | Theological anthropology--Christianity. |
  Christian ethics.
Classification: LCC BT695.5 .W564 2017 | DDC 202/.12--dc23 LC record
available at https://lccn.loc.gov/2017009102

Cover design and layout by Margaret Ryland
Front cover image: Kevin Eaves / Shutterstock.com

Table of Contents

ACKNOWLEDGMENTS   VII

CHAPTER 1
Catholic Ecology?   1

CHAPTER 2
The Mastery of Nature . . . Including Human
Nature   11

CHAPTER 3
Empire of Waste   31

CHAPTER 4
Dehumanization and Food Pollution   59

CHAPTER 5:
The Pollution of Sex   95

CHAPTER 6
The Global Warming Debate   127

CHAPTER 7
The Great Pyramid of Beings, Natural Law,
the Ecological Hierarchy, and Your Own
Ecosystem   163

CHAPTER 8
Getting Back to Nature   193

CONCLUSION   239

Acknowledgments

I would like to thank Franciscan University for its support in writing this book, especially Daniel Kempton, Stephen Krason, and Paul Symington. I also thank Logan Gage and Eric Haenni who read the chapter on global warming (although any errors or confusions that remain are mine). I was also aided greatly by our department's research assistant, Valerie Wark. And finally, I'd like to thank my dear wife Teri for reading over the manuscript, and Anna Wiker-Piecynski for making valuable suggestions. *Ad maiorem Dei gloriam.*

CHAPTER ONE

Catholic Ecology?

The first thing one thinks upon seeing the title of this first chapter, *Catholic Ecology*, is, of course, "Is there such a thing as a Catholic Ecology?" The phrase conjures up something like a very dull and soon-to-be dusty treatise that gathers together anything a pope, a saint, or an official Church document has ever said that remotely pertains to taking care of the environment, the goodness of creation, stewardship principles, or making happy with the birds like St. Francis.

Such a book may exist, and it would certainly be useful if it did, but this is not that book. This book, as the title indicates, is about the Catholic unity of environmental, economic, and moral ecology—in short, catholic ecology with a small "c." The original, etymological meaning of "catholic," from the Greek καθολικός, is "universal," as in, entirely comprehensive. On this understanding, "catholic" ecology is defined by a concern for all of nature, including human nature and hence what we may call Moral Ecology as well. What is obviously significant in this book's argument is the expansion of our understanding of ecology from its current focus on nature out there—trees, rivers, oceans, animals, birds, the air, distinct ecosystems, etc.— to include what should be an obvious part of nature that has been, for some reason, mysteriously left out of the environmental movement: human nature and human morality.

I am not denying that there is such a thing as Catholic Ecology with a big "C." In fact, unbeknownst to many Catholics and non-Catholics alike, the Catholic Church already accepts this expanded understanding of ecology which includes both nature and human nature. The doctrine of creation, defining creation as good and human nature as part of that creation as very good, has been part of the Catholic understanding from the beginning; it has its roots in the Old Testament and branches in the New.

In regard to the Old Testament, the Psalmists, generally speaking, are tree huggers, mountain huggers, and, insofar as is possible, stream huggers, because all creation sings the glory of the Creator, and so the Psalmists regularly sing the glory of creation. There is a very simple rule in this Israelite ecology: you can hug the cedars of Lebanon all you want; just do not carve them into gods.

But of course, the New Testament affirms the glories of creation, of nature, even more radically, since it is revealed that God Himself, God the Son, became incarnate in nature, uniting Himself with human nature, and it was the Son through whom all things were made, both nature and human nature.

Finally, the Church itself has said a lot about the intrinsic goodness of creation, and there is a rich history of theological reflection, including reflections by popes and saints, on understanding our proper relationship to creation, to nature, that is, to what has been called "the environment." Of course, there is St. Francis, and also Pope Francis' *Laudato si'*, as the latest offering.

As I said, someone may well have written a book on Catholic Ecology and written it well, but that is not this book. *In Defense of Nature: The Catholic Unity of Environmental, Economic, and Moral Ecology* is about catholic ecology in the first sense; that is, catholic with a small "c," because I am offering an argument that can be understood and appreciated by all, and in doing so, some common ground can be established on what has hitherto been a battleground between the Left and the Right, Liberals and Conservatives, about the extremely touchy and volatile subject of Ecology.

My argument is very simple, at least in outline, containing four seemingly logical steps:

1. Just as there is an order of nature which is good, wonderful, and beautiful that we should both respect and protect, so also there is an order of human nature which is good, wonderful, and beautiful, and we should respect and protect that, too.

2. When we violate the order of nature in some way, we generally call that "pollution," meaning by this that we have in some way by our actions damaged nature—whether it is the air, the water, or some particular species.

3. If human nature is indeed, as its name suggests, part of nature, then we should be able to call violations of the order of human nature "moral pollution," and for the very same reason we can claim that we have in some way by our actions damaged human nature—whether it is our body, our sexual nature, some other aspect of our moral nature, or our capacity to freely choose what is good.

4. Therefore, our understanding of ecology should be expanded to include respect for and protection of both nature and human nature; in short, our ecology should be catholic, universal, including both environmental ecology and moral ecology, and whatever connections we find between them.

Establishing ourselves as moral beings by nature is good for us and good for the environment. If we are in fact moral beings by nature—meaning not that we are naturally good, but that we are the one peculiar animal who has to both know and choose well in order to act well in regard to ourselves and to nature—then we can be held morally accountable for what we do to our own nature and to the environment. On this expanded understanding of ecology, it is immoral to dump destructive chemicals like meth into our bodies or destroy our sexual nature with pornography, and it is immoral to dump destructive chemicals into the air or destroy ecosystems for our trivial pleasures.

One would think—or, should I say, I have foolishly thought—that this expanded account of ecology would be so obvious as to be accepted without argument. Not so, alas. There is a significant obstacle facing the acceptance of catholic ecology in this sense: the deep cultural and intellectual divide between the Left and the Right, between Liberals and Conservatives.

I'm fairly certain the reader will know what I am referring to, but in case not, I shall offer a broad brushstroke picture of the two sides, quick characterizations that are bordering on caricatures, to make the problem both visible and vivid. I realize that characterizations, or going a bit further, caricatures, have their dangers, but they are often instructive overgeneralizations that give us clues (if even by exaggeration) to the common prejudices and dearly held opinions of rival parties that stand in the way of accepting the whole truth about something.

In regard to the environment, the Left sees those on the Right as self-righteous, woman-hating, Bible-thumping, voracious consumer-capitalists, ripping up millions of trees and throwing down endless miles of pavement so they can tank around from mall to mall in their gas-guzzling SUVs, spewing fast-food trash out of their tinted electric windows while they sing "God Bless America" and blithely plow over innocent animals who haplessly wander onto their asphalt paths.

The Right sees the Left as atheistic, human-hating, earth-worshiping socialists who eat funny food, drive politically correct toy cars, and spend their time saving whales and nearly invisible and obscure creek creatures, even while they heartily support abortion, euthanasia, gay marriage, and even the collective extermination of the human species for the sake of saving the natural environment (especially the CCC—Caucasian Christian Capitalists).

You can tell where you are, in regard to your own view of things, by which characterization you find amusing and accurate, and which one you find offensive. I find them both amusing and I find them both offensive, and unfortunately, lamentably accurate.

These characterizations tell us just as much about the targets of the barbs as those who cast them, both what they see and what are their respective blind spots. It's the kind of half-clear vision—seeing the splinter in the other's eye but not the beam in one's own—that creates the distorted vision that the Left and Right have of each other in regard to the environment. The whole environment, the natural *and* moral environment, the entire natural bundle, is included in a truly catholic ecology.

The goal of this book is to clear up the vision of both sides so we can bring ourselves, and our modern society, out of this back-and-forth-but-getting-nowhere stalemate (a condition Pope Francis, in his environmental encyclical *Laudato si'*, called our "constant schizophrenia"[1]).

Clearing up our vision of the environment is not an easy task. Because of ingrained habits of thinking on both sides, we need to proceed slowly. So, let's leave at least a little of the above caricatures behind and move to more accurate characterizations, restating things a bit more clearly about the typical opinions on both sides.

The Left is typically deeply concerned about the natural environment but often considers human nature to be an invasive if not evil presence in an otherwise paradisal garden. The Right is typically deeply concerned about human nature, but is either indifferent or even hostile to concern for the natural environment. So, while the Left is obsessed with pollution of the natural environment, the Right is obsessed with pollution of the moral environment. The unpleasant and obfuscating result is that each refuses to see the other's legitimate claims to truth because the other side seems to be tied inextricably to evident error.

The Right looks at the Left and thinks, "All those who are so hyped up about environmentalism are also rabidly pro-abortion and pro-gay marriage, *and therefore their concern about the natural environment must be essentially corrupt too.*" The Left looks at the Right and thinks, "All

---

[1]   Pope Francis, Encyclical Letter on Care for Our Common Home *Laudato si'* (May 24, 2015), §118.

those who are so hyped up about abortion and homosexuality are also rabidly destroying not just the beauty of our natural environment, but poisoning the water and land as well, *and therefore their concern about 'morality' must be essentially corrupt, too."*

Guilt by association, so to speak. And so each side is satisfied with a half-truth as the whole truth. Half-truths are easy to digest because, like picky eaters, one chooses only those items on the whole plate of truth that fit one's palate.

What if the whole truth would actually be the addition of the two halves, or more accurately, a whole lot more than the sum of these two parts?

But such a thought seems unthinkable to each side of our divided house, and so confusion reigns and thus rains on the common ground of the public square where a good conversation could actually take place.

The problem is not only what each side wants to avoid, but what each side pursues as progress. Many on the Left tend to believe (even though they proclaim the inviolable integrity of nature) that there are no intrinsic, inviolable natural moral limits defining the integrity of human nature, so that progress means being able to do whatever we want with human nature. Many on the Right (even though they proclaim the inviolable moral integrity of human nature) tend to believe that there are no intrinsic, inviolable limits to our use of nature, so that progress means being able to do whatever we want with nature. Each side's progress is the other's poison. The result (as already noted) is intractable animosity and cultural deadlock.

Are these overgeneralizations? Caricatures? Yes, but instructively so, because even though quickly sketched and therefore somewhat cartoonish, they are based upon recognizably real characters in our society which most of us resemble—some more, and some less.

Very few take the astounding position that there is both a natural ecology and a moral ecology, and that these two are intimately interdependent. As I noted briefly above, that is, in fact, the Catholic Church's position, and it has been for two thousand years. According to Catholic doctrine, nature is good *and* human nature is good, and each has its own inviolable limits that must be respected. But, sadly, those limits are not being respected today, and have not been for some time. The result is that there is now both significant natural and moral pollution, and they both have a single cause: the human will running roughshod over nature in one way or the other.

Even more telling, as we shall demonstrate, moral pollution and environmental pollution are inextricably linked. This is necessarily the case because human *nature* is part of nature, even while it transcends nature. If you poison the air and the water, you poison yourself. If you reject the necessity of moral virtue (say, temperance, for example) and embrace a wasteful life of consumerist luxury, then you create inverted mountains of toxic trash in landfills. If you indiscriminately tinker with varied genetic modifications or foolishly introduce species to or extinguish species from delicate ecologies, you invite unpredictable natural disasters. If you indiscriminately tinker with sexuality or introduce endless sexual variation or extinguish natural sexual practices from the delicate human moral ecology, you invite equivalent disasters in regard to human nature.

The Left understands the exquisite, delicate harmony of the natural order. The Right understands the exquisite delicate harmony of the moral order. Each side will tell you how very little a deviation it takes to cause disaster to the natural or moral order. But each refuses to see the other's argument.

All that is needed to heal our present divisions is simply this: that each sees what the other sees so clearly, and how it all fits together. And that is what *In Defense of Nature* is about: the restoration of the proper sense of ecology to include both nature and human nature, natural ecology and moral ecology. Hence the subtitle of this book: *The Catholic Unity of Environmental, Economic, and Moral Ecology.*

No small task. We'll begin by going back to the historical root of the problem, a common root that may surprise those on both the Left and Right.

CHAPTER TWO

The Mastery Of Nature . . . Including Human Nature

Two Sides of Bacon

Several centuries ago, there arose a new way to approach nature. Nature was not, as it had been considered within Christianity and Judaism (and for certain pagan authors as well), a wisely-made and beautifully interconnected order with its own integrity. Rather, nature was cast as a kind of enemy, something that opposed us, and hence had to be conquered by human technical power for the sake of human comfort, convenience, pleasure, health, and longevity. On this new view, nature was therefore to be treated as clay in the human potter's hands, to be molded as we wished. The goal of this self-consciously new philosophy was (if we might borrow one of its main architect's words) to "make ourselves . . . masters and possessors of nature."[1]

These are the words of the famous French philosopher René Descartes (1596–1650). His intellectual mentor, Francis Bacon (1561–1626), initiated the project to master nature which Descartes happily took up. Bacon was even more explicit and grandiose in his claims about his new

---

[1] René Descartes, *Discourse on Method*, trans. Richard Kennington (Newburyport, MA: Focus Publishing), Part 6, 49.

science. "I am laboring to lay the foundation, not of any sect or doctrine, but of human utility and power," Bacon declared boldly.[2] For Bacon, the "goal of the sciences is none other than this: that human life be endowed with new discoveries and powers," so that "man [may] endeavor to establish and extend the power and dominion of the human race itself over the universe" in an "empire of man over things."[3]

Not a small project, imperial mastery of the universe and all things in it. The ambiguity inherent in this new technocratic mastery of everything is twofold.

First, granted we can dominate nature via technology as Bacon hoped, do we as human beings truly have the *wisdom* to understand all the ramifications of our ever-increasing technological power? Or will our technical power advance beyond our grasp of the deep intricacies of nature, so we will end up destroying ourselves by destroying nature upon which we depend?

Second, what does it mean to extend technical mastery of nature to human nature? And just who will end up being the master of whom and for what ends?

These are the essential questions that arise from the Baconian project. How does this all fit in with the previous chapter's discussion about the typical opinions of the Left and Right about ecology broadly considered, including both environmental and moral ecology?

Recalling that we were making use of helpful overgen-

---

[2] Francis Bacon, *The Great Instauration* in *The New Organon and Related Writings*, ed. Fulton Anderson (New York: Macmillan Publishing Company, 1988), 16.

[3] Francis Bacon, *The New Organon* in *The New Organon and Related Writings*; I, aphorisms lxxxi and cxxix. See also Francis Bacon, *The New Organon*, aphorisms cxvi–cxvii, cxxix.

eralizations, we can say that the Left cringes at the first kind of mastery. Concerned as it is about the natural environment, it is highly critical of the Baconian dream (shared by many since) to overpower nature through technology and industry because the unbridled striving for such dominion leads to the pollution of rivers, lakes, and air; to the destruction of natural habitats and precious species; and to the disgraceful utilitarian treatment of nature as a mere instrument of human pleasure and convenience; all without regard to the consequences for the beauty, integrity, and stability of the order of the natural world.

The key complaint of the Left—and it is quite legitimate—is that while technology does indeed give us power over nature, we human beings often lack the wisdom, the larger and deeper understanding of nature, to use that power well. Therefore, we trample the inherent limits and intricate order of nature, and the result is unwitting or wanton destruction of the environment, which foolishly leads to human degradation and self-destruction as well, since we depend on the environment.

The Right cringes at the second kind of mastery, the mastery of human nature. Concerned as it is with what it considers an ever more degraded moral environment, the Right is highly critical of the Baconian dream of technologically mastering human nature because that dominion leads to the disgraceful utilitarian treatment of human beings or parts of their bodies as mere instruments of pleasure and convenience regardless of the moral, psychological, social, or physical consequences.

The key complaint of the Right—and it is quite legitimate—is that while technology does indeed give us greater and greater power over human nature, we human beings often lack the wisdom, the larger and deeper understanding of our own nature, to use that power well. Therefore, we trample the inherent limits and intricate moral order of human nature, and the result is unwitting or wanton self-destruction.

Each side understands half of the problem with Bacon's grand project, but ignores or downplays the side of Bacon the other takes seriously. Thus, each points to the ill effects, the evident destruction, that supports its own side, but overlooks or dismisses the glaring evidence offered by the other side that calls into question its own cherished assumptions.

What would it look like to take both sides seriously? That's just what we'll do in this and the following chapters, adding Left to Right so we get the whole picture. In order for this to be more effective, we'll need to do a bit of a deeper analysis of Bacon's entire argument to set things up more securely.

The Whole Hog

Francis Bacon stands at the very head of the modern project aimed at mastering nature through technology and industry, and he is generally regarded as one of the great founders of modern science. While he didn't contribute much to the actual technical project of mastering nature except his rousing words that initiated it, these words were arguably the most powerful catalyst driving the project forward from the beginning.

However, to give a proper account of Bacon's new philosophy of nature, we have to go back to a previous, even more notorious thinker, the great founder of modern political philosophy, Niccolò Machiavelli (1469–1527). There should be no doubt that Machiavelli was modernity's first great atheist, and it must be acknowledged that Bacon read and largely approved of Machiavelli.[4]

As many have noted, there are particularly striking parallel passages where Bacon applies Machiavelli's famous words about the rape of Fortuna (the fickle goddess of chance) to nature itself. Why does Machiavelli invoke such an objectionable image as the rape of a woman to advance his new understanding of politics, or realpolitik, as we now term politics guided by amoral pragmatism?

For Machiavelli, God does not rule human affairs, fortune does. But it need not be so. We can force fortune to bend to our wishes if we are willing to bend the rules. Hence, in regard to Lady Fortune, Machiavelli declares,

> I judge this indeed, that it is better to be impetuous than cautious, because fortune is a woman; and it is necessary, if one wants to hold her down, to beat her and strike her down. And one sees that she lets herself be won more by the impetuous

---

[4] I say there should be no doubt because there are in fact scholars who try to make a case for the notorious Machiavelli's piety. I side with the obvious conclusion that a man who counsels that princes should be free to do any evil act, and even use religion as a ruse to gain political power, cannot be anything other than, well, Machiavellian—a teacher of evil. In this debate, I side with Leo Strauss. See his *Thoughts on Machiavelli* (Chicago: University of Chicago Press, 1984 reprint), 9. Bacon was a careful reader of Machiavelli, and not shy about referring to him, given the number of times he quotes from both *The Prince* and *Discourses on Livy*, and he did so with no hint of disapproval. Thus, e.g., see his *The Advancement of Learning* in Francis Bacon, *The Major Works*, ed. Brian Vickers (Oxford: University of Oxford Press, 1996), II, 270–271, 279, 282, 284. See also Bacon's essay, "Of Goodness and Goodness of Nature," which gives an intriguing off-hand affirmation of Machiavelli's assessment of Christianity as hampered by its own goodness in being effective (contained in *The Major Works*, 363–364).

than by those who proceed coldly. And so always, like a woman, she is the friend of the young, because they are less cautious, more ferocious, and command her with more audacity.[5]

Part of that audacity, the greatest part, is that the Machiavellian prince must be willing to do evil when it is necessary or beneficial to his gaining or maintaining political power. "For a man who wants to make a profession of good in all regards must come to ruin among so many who are not good. Hence it is necessary to a prince, if he wants to maintain himself, to learn to be able *not to be good*, and to use this and not use it according to necessity."[6]

We now see the connection to Machiavelli's atheism. It should be obvious that a prince who is willing to do evil to gain or stay in power cannot be worried about the fate of his immortal soul; therefore, Machiavelli's teaching about what makes for political success for a prince contains an implicit denial of Christianity. Political power *in this life* is all that matters, and political power is gained by the audacious use of power, stripped of any moral inhibitions.

Bacon borrows this violent imagery to make clear to his readers that nature itself must be treated the same way that Machiavelli treats fortune—with impetuous force. To be more exact, nature must be examined not just as it freely presents itself, but even more, under man-imposed duress. In his somewhat antiquated terms, Bacon calls for a new "natural history," that is, a *new* examination of nature and collection of facts:

---

[5] Niccolò Machiavelli, *The Prince*, trans. Harvey Mansfield (Chicago: University of Chicago Press, 1985), XXV, 101.

[6] Machiavelli, XV, 61. Emphasis added.

With regard to the mass and composition of it:
I mean it to be a history not only of nature free
and at large (when she is left to her own course
and does her work her way) . . . but much more
of nature under constraint and vexed; that is
to say, when by art and the hands of man she is
forced out of her natural state, and squeezed and
moulded. . . . [For] the nature of things betrays
itself more readily under the vexations of art
than in its natural freedom.[7]

---

[7] Bacon, *The Great Instauration*, 25. See also Bacon, *The New Organon*, aphorism xcviii. Bacon makes a witty, if ribald, connection to Machiavelli's abuse of the goddess Fortuna. "Certainly what is said of opportunity or fortune is most true of nature: she has a lock in front, but is bald behind" (Bacon, *The New Organon*, aphorism cxxi). This saying originally refers to a god, not a goddess, Caerus, who represents opportunity. Men may grasp the single lock of hair Caerus has in the front, but will miss their chance if they try to snatch him as he runs by them, given that the back of his head is bald. On Bacon's use of rape imagery as a new approach to nature, see Carolyn Merchant, *The Death of Nature: Women, Ecology, and the Scientific Revolution* (San Francisco: Harper Collins, 1989), 164–172. For a more detailed, complex account of Bacon's view of nature, as related the vexations of art, see Sophie Weeks, "Francis Bacon and the Art-Nature Distinction," *Ambix* 54, no. 2 (2007): 101–129. Some have tried to finesse Bacon's distinction of art vs. nature, in regard to mastery, and see him only proposing technology, art, as a grand imitation of nature—but I would add, one that puts technological man in the place of God. See J. Peter Zetterberg, "Echoes of Nature in Salomon's House," *Journal of the History of Ideas* 43, no. 2 (1982): 179–193. There are those who, on a more general level, have reinterpreted Bacon's relationship to nature far more benevolently, a position I also find unconvincing. See, for example, Peter Pesic, "Francis Bacon, Violence, and the Motion of Liberty: The Aristotelian Background," *Journal of the History of Ideas* 75, no. 1 (2014): 69–89; Pesic "Wrestling with Proteus: Francis Bacon and the 'Torture' of Nature," *Isis* 90 (1999): 81–94; and Iddo Landau, "Feminist Criticisms of Metaphors in Bacon's Philosophy of Science," *Philosophy* 73 (1998): 47–61. For the back-and-forth between the two sides, largely defined in terms of feminist critiques of Bacon, see Brian Vickers, "Francis Bacon, Feminist Historiography, and the Dominion of Nature," *Journal of the History of Ideas* 69, no. 1 (2008): 117–141; Katharine

The connection between Machiavelli's treatment of fortune and Bacon's domination of nature is this: for Bacon, nature *as it presents itself freely* is, in large part, the cause of our bad fortune, or misfortunes, as human beings. Nature isn't intrinsically good. It doesn't give us endless bounty and health, but famine, disease, and ultimately, mortality. To get what *we* want, we must reject the notion that nature is good, and force out of her the goods we desire.

Like Machiavelli, Bacon bids his followers to push beyond the Christian view of goodness, and to do whatever it takes to master our fate and fortunes in this world by mastering nature. This mastering of nature through human art, that is, technology, will (promises Bacon) result in "a line and race of inventions that may in some degree subdue and overcome the necessities and miseries of humanity."[8]

The goal of Bacon's new science, then, is entirely practical and this-worldly. This new science does not aim at the contemplation of the beautiful order of nature as it freely presents itself—that is, at the contemplation of the wonders of God's creation. Instead, "the true and lawful goal of the sciences is none other than this: that human life be endowed with new discoveries and powers."[9]

The goal of his science is therefore purely utilitarian. In fact, "Truth, therefore, and utility are here the very same

---

Park, "Response to Brian Vickers, 'Francis Bacon, Feminist Historiography, and the Dominion of Nature,'" *Journal of the History of Ideas* 69, no. 1 (2008): 143–146; and Carolyn Merchant, "The Secrets of Nature: The Bacon Debates Revisited," *Journal of the History of Ideas* 69, no. 1, (2008): 147–162.

8   Ibid., 23.

9   Bacon, *The New Organon*, aphorism lxxxi. See also *The Great Instauration*, 29.

things" because the entire aim of the new science is "to over-come . . . nature."[10] Subduing nature is the only "argument" that counts, a work "which cannot be done without a very diligent dissection and anatomy of the world."[11] Nature must be taken apart, so we might rebuild it according to our desires.

As with Machiavelli, there is an implicit atheism, insofar as Bacon's treatment of nature implies that—in contrast to the Genesis account accepted at the time—nature is not good. Like fortune in political affairs, nature itself opposes us, hampers our happiness in this life, causes us misery, and will continue to do so until we take the ini-tiative and force nature to conform to our desires.

Of course, Bacon realized the obvious Christian ob-jection to treating nature as something to be vexed or tortured rather than contemplated and admired as the work of a wise and beneficent Creator, and was at sig-nificant pains to explain how his new science was not sacrilegious.[12] If nature is created good, why vex her rather than be content to admire her wonders? It would seem, given the Judeo-Christian affirmation of the es-sential goodness of nature, that the forceful "inquisition of nature" would therefore be "interdicted or forbidden," a point Bacon himself brings up, but then rather casually (and disingenuously) dismisses.[13]

---

[10] Ibid., aphorism cxxiv and Author's Preface, p. 36. See also *The Great Instauration*, 19.

[11] Ibid., aphorisms cxxiv and li.

[12] See ibid., aphorism lxxxix.

[13] Upon warning against the "error" of thinking "that the inquisition of nature is in any part interdicted or forbidden," Bacon asserted that human beings, in the Genesis account, were punished only for the am-bitious and proud desire to define good and evil themselves, and not for inquiry into nature—thereby obscuring the kind of ruthless inquiry he was proposing (Ibid., 15).

One rightly wonders (and many scholars have) about his religious sincerity here.[14] In regard to this oft-asked question of Bacon's religious sincerity, let's not forget the obvious. His project shifts humanity's main efforts *away* from the Christian concern about the fate of the soul in the next world *toward* bodily comfort and long life in this world. As he makes especially clear in his imaginative essay, *New Atlantis*, the human needs that the project of the mastery of nature promises are very, very worldly. In fact, he seems to be replacing what Christians are promised in heaven in the next world with a kind of techno-utopia in this world.

This is not a tenuous inference on my part. In *New Atlantis*, Bacon sketches out a fictional research institute called Salomon's House, a kind of scientific work-tank which is meant to convey his aspirations about the project of conquering nature. "The end of our Foundation [Salomon's House] is the knowledge of Causes, and secret motions of things; and the enlarging of the bounds of Human Empire, to the effecting of all things possible."[15]

This imaginary project hardly rings of Christian humility; rather, it sounds like the greatest pride. But before we judge Bacon, we ought to look at what he promises the human race if it follows his lead.

---

[14] On the question of Bacon's religious sincerity, especially as he relies on Machiavelli, see Richard Kennington, "Bacon's Humanitarian Revision of Machiavelli," in *On Modern Origins: Essays in Early Modern Philosophy*, ed. Pamela Kraus and Frank Hunt (Lanham, MD: Lexington Books, 2004); Paul Rahe, *Republics Ancient & Modern*, vol. 2, *New Modes and Orders in Early Modern Political Thought* (Chapel Hill, NC: University of North Carolina Press, 1994), 44–52; and Timothy Paterson, "On the Role of Christianity in the Political Philosophy of Francis Bacon," *Polity* 19, no. 3, (1987): 419–442.

[15] See Francis Bacon, *New Atlantis*, in *The Major Works*, 480.

In his fictional account, Bacon's Salomon's House produces new artificial metals, invents refrigeration, creates engines to harness the wind, makes "artificial wells and fountains"—one of which, by the infusion of "many things," will be a "Water of Paradise" that will bring "health, and prolongation of life." The House also produces artificial rain and snow, thunder and lightning. There are "Chambers of Health" to cure "divers[e] diseases," orchards and gardens improved by human art so that "their fruit [is] greater and sweeter and of differing taste, smell, colour, and figure from their nature." It also makes "divers[e] new plants," and has "parks and enclosures of all sorts of beasts and birds," not just to view but even more importantly, "for dissections and trials" upon the animals that may bring us physical improvements that "may be wrought upon the body of man," including the "resuscitating of some [human beings] that seem dead in appearance. . . ." The House also breeds new creatures by "commixtures and copulations" of different kinds of animals, as well as creates entirely novel creatures—serpents, worms, flies, and fish—by "putrefaction" (spontaneous generation from rotting material, as those in the time thought occurred with maggots in garbage). Its scientists also build "spectacles and glasses" to see "objects afar off, as in the heaven," as well as to "see small and minute bodies perfectly and distinctly. . . ." They produce "artificial rain-bows" and new "precious stones," as well as create sound machines to imitate all natural sounds, perfumes to "imitate smells," and concoctions to "deceive any man's taste." There are "engine-houses" that produce weapons "stronger, and more violent" than any heretofore known by man, "instruments of war" which entail "new mixtures and compositions of gun-powder," some of which produce "wildfires burning in water" that are "unquenchable. . . ."

There is even a house within Salomon's House dedicated to producing "deceits of the senses . . . false apparitions, impostures, and illusions. . . ."[16]

Appended to *New Atlantis* was a list of desirable discoveries, so that readers could canvass quickly the kind of useful goods Bacon was promising if only nature were squeezed long and diligently enough by the vexations of the new scientists. To quote some:

The prolongation of life.
The restitution of youth in some degree.
The retardation of age.
The curing of diseases counted incurable.
The mitigation of pain.
The increasing of strength and activity.
The increasing of ability to suffer torture and pain.
The altering of complexions [bodily characteristics], and fatness and leanness.
The altering of statures [physical size].
The altering of features [of the face].
The increasing and exalting of the intellectual parts.
Versions [transformations] of bodies into other bodies.
Making of new species.
Transplanting of one species into another.
Instruments of destruction, as of war and poison.
Exhilaration of the spirits, and putting them in good disposition.
[R]aising of tempests.
Making new threads for apparel . . .
Deceptions of the senses.
Greater pleasures of the senses.

[16] Bacon, *New Atlantis*, 471–488.

There we have it—Bacon's dream House, a very this-worldly enterprise that bends science to the service of earthly utility, pleasure, power, and even amusement. Few things in his description seem as fanciful now as they no doubt did in the early seventeenth century. In fact, for the most part, we've far surpassed Bacon's wildest dreams of mastery.

For that reason, much of what Bacon suggested is unobjectionable to us, perhaps even laudable, on first reading. Telescopes, microscopes, metallurgy, animal breeding, plant enhancement, artificial fabrics like nylon or polyester, plastic surgery, pain medicine, the curing of diseases. Some might cringe at the animal dissections, or the indiscriminate attempts to manipulate animal species by breeding and who knows what else—something like our Genetically Modified Organisms (GMOs). Some others might be ambivalent about plastic surgery, Prozac, liposuction, the hyper-titillation of the senses, the chemical search for the fountain of youth, or possibly even a transhumanist technological remaking of humanity itself. More will shake their heads in regret at the goal of mastering nature to create ever more powerful "instruments of war." A few, thinking a bit more deeply, will wonder who might be using the power of deceiving the senses by creating illusions and apparitions, and upon whom and for what ends. And what about the power of conjuring up tempests? A plaything for the hyper-rich? For tyrants? For mischievous or nihilistic youth?

These questions are serious enough. But we again need to remind ourselves, in our overall assessment of Bacon's project as it has played out in the almost four centuries since its inception, that he believes his new science of mastering nature applies to human nature as well—"I certainly mean what I have said to be understood" not just about nature out there, but also "logic, ethics, and politics. . . ."[17] This has an odor of technological totalitarianism and social engineering, if even along the less brutal but no less dehumanizing lines of *Brave New World.*

Whether Bacon himself envisioned technology as a means for totalitarian political control, the union of utilitarian technical mastery of nature and human nature that forms the foundations of Bacon's proposed political utopia in his *New Atlantis* is explicitly aimed at a new transpolitical, humanitarian end: to create a this-worldly utopia where all our pains have been conquered, all our pleasures are being ever more greatly enhanced, and the common aim of the complete technological control of nature unites all of humanity. Technological power and plenty, universally spread, displaces the particularity of politics—just as Karl Marx would envision two centuries after Bacon. When this wonderful utopian stage is reached, then "man is a god to man,"[18] that is, the Baconian master is—to all previous ages and to all under his power—exactly what previous ages thought God to be: an all-powerful and (one assumes) wise and good being. This techno-utopian Baconian god rules benevolently over both nature and human nature.

That vision raises the obvious question, doesn't it, after four centuries: Can human beings be trusted with ever more god-like power? It certainly seems that there is no essential union in human beings of power, wisdom, and goodness, as Bacon seems to have counted on. Instead,

---

[17] Bacon, *The New Organon*, aphorism cxxvii. See also aphorism cxxix.
[18] Ibid., aphorism cxxix.

even as we have developed more and more god-like power, we find that technological power is being used both wisely and foolishly, for good and for evil, for environmental enhancement and for destruction, for human flourishing and for degradation. It's a mixed bag, and the more powerful the technology, the more powerful and confusing the mix.

We'll get to that mix in the next chapters. Here, we must end with an extraordinarily important point. The new science put forth by Bacon is, as we noted, implicitly atheistic. Independently of whether Bacon himself was or was not being duplicitous about his belief in God, the driving force of his notion of mastery of nature is that nature is entirely materialistically defined: that is, soul-free. As Paul Rahe rightly notes, "Bacon's scientific revolution was to put the body, its needs, and the prolongation of man's earthly life at the center of human affairs. Regarding the noble work of fostering the health of the soul, he had little or nothing to say." We become gods by our manipulation of nature for our material benefit, seeking pleasure and immortality of, and in, the body. In so deliberately elevating the goods of the body, Bacon thereby "laid the foundation for a radical, this-worldly redirection of the Christian faith,"[19] one that, if its developed trajectory continues as it has these last two centuries, would seem to end in Christianity's extinction in a completely secularized world.

But this isn't just about the fate of Christianity. Bacon's project as it has played out should shock, and perhaps awaken, both the Left and the Right.

To begin with the Left, it means that the ever more intense desire to dominate and manipulate nature that

---

defines so much of the abuse of our natural world is rooted in the rejection of the reality of the soul (and at least implicitly in a rejection or radical malformation of Christianity). It is because we view our only home as *here* and our only pleasures as *now* that we seek so frantically to extract from nature anything and everything for our comfort and convenience. The ultimate historical and philosophical source of our modern rape of the environment—recall Machiavelli's and Bacon's imagery—is modern atheism. But the Left, including those most concerned about environmental degradation, are almost invariably secular-minded materialists who reject both God and the soul.

Here, some on the Left might object and reply that the real historical source of the desire to master nature came from a combination of two Genesis passages, the first where God, having created man and woman, blesses them, and bids them, "Be fruitful and multiply, and fill the earth and subdue it; and have dominion over the fish of the sea and over the birds of the air and over every living thing that moves upon the earth" (Gen 1:28), and the second where, after they sin, God punishes Adam and Eve, and hence all human beings to come, with earthly existence filled with pain, toil, thorns, and thistles, instead of a blissful life in a garden (Gen 3:16–19). The notion is that, somehow, Christianity therefore heartily affirms feverishly subduing the earth and exercising despot-like dominion over it—an effort all the more excusable on account of the wreck of nature caused by sin that makes us have to labor, drenched with the sweat of our brows, for our daily bread.[20]

---

[20] This is the so-called Lynn White thesis, sparked by White's essay, "The Historical Roots of Our Ecological Crisis," in David Spring and Eileen

That is, however, a perversion of Christian orthodoxy—one that can be traced, in no small part, to Francis Bacon. As Rahe and others have argued convincingly, Bacon well understood that, in his Christian-dominated time, he could not put forth his radical ideas without couching them in Christian terms, otherwise he would be persecuted for atheism. Following Machiavelli's counsels about dissembling—appearing to be religious in public while engaging in irreligious activities behind the scenes[21]—Bacon inserted his worldly secular project into what appears to be a Christian shell.[22] On this interpretation—which I share—Bacon *used* Christianity, redirected it for his own, this-worldly purposes.

Sadly, many on the Right who are Christians have swallowed Bacon's utilitarian transformation of Christianity without asking some rather obvious questions. First and foremost is this: how can the intense focus on a this-worldly techno-economic utopia, catering entirely to the comforts, pleasures, and conveniences of the body, be reconciled with the Christian renunciation of the world and the embrace of the cross? Or with the Christian championing of the essential virtue of humility (vs. the hubristic desire to create a human empire over all things with god-like control of nature)? Or with the very Christian virtue of temperance (which aims for a moder-

---

Spring, eds., *Ecology and Religion in History* (New York: Harper, 1974), 15–31.

[21] See Machiavelli, XVIII.

[22] Along with Rahe, see Paterson, "On the Role of Christianity in the Political Philosophy of Francis Bacon"; Jerry Weinberger, *Science, Faith, and Politics: Francis Bacon and the Utopian Roots of the Modern Age* (Ithaca, NY: Cornell University Press, 1985); and Kimberly Hurd Hale, *Francis Bacon's New Atlantis in the Foundation of Modern Political Thought* (Lanham, MD: Lexington Books, 2013).

ate use of this world's bodily goods)? Or, again, with the
Judeo-Christian understanding that creation is good and
manifests the wisdom of the Creator?

And that should give the Right pause to consider some
deeper points. The embrace of materialism was the pre-
condition for the modern frantic, immoderate pursuit of
technological, industrial, and economic development. For
Christians, and key pagans as well (such as Plato, Aristotle,
and Cicero), the passionate attachment to material goods,
the liberation of greed from any censure so that economic development could speed forward, the endless appeal
to the pleasure of the senses and absorption in material
comfort and convenience, the infinitude of trivial distractions that numb the intellect, *were all things to be avoided as
degrading of the higher goods of the soul.* The result, if these
worldly things are embraced, will be the enervation and
even eclipse of the soul, an effect which breeds a kind of
practical atheism in neglecting the soul and God for far
lesser goods, and which fosters hedonism which swallows up Christian morality. On top of all this, treating
creation, the environment, irreverently—and what could
be more irreverent than rape as the standard-bearing
image?—would seem to be an affront to the Creator. Such
treatment would be understandable from an atheist who
thought that the pleasures of this life were all there were
to be had, and that nature was the result of a purposeless
swirl of matter and energy. But how can it be reconciled
with Christianity?

So, it would appear that the Left and the Right both
have something to think about: the Left, that the environmental degradation it despises might, ironically, be
rooted in atheism, in the secular rejection of Christianity
that ultimately forms the typical ideas of the Left; and

the Right, that its indifference and even hostility to environmental concerns and its unambiguous affirmation of the techno-economic project of remaking nature to suit our this-worldly comfort have more in common with the atheist Bacon than the incarnate Christ.

With that in mind, let's look in more detail some of the ill effects of the Baconian project that both sides, Left and Right, need to hear about. We will examine the deeply interconnected environmental and moral pollution that results from our attempts to master nature and human nature as if we ourselves were gods.

CHAPTER THREE

Empire of Waste

Wall·E *World*

One of the most entertaining and profound reflections on the Baconian project of creating a New Atlantis is the Pixar classic, *Wall·E* (2008). In *Wall·E*, we get a vivid picture of what it might mean for human beings to attempt to make a techno-economic utopia on Earth where nature is entirely mastered for human comfort and convenience (with robots doing all the work). The result is dystopian rather than utopian. This mastery has not only, quite literally, trashed Earth itself, but fundamentally dehumanized human beings who now wander homeless in space.[1]

I do not intend to tire the reader with a detailed analysis of *Wall·E*, but I will use the basic themes of the movie to help begin our deeper examination of ecology in the

---

[1] It is interesting to our analysis of *Wall·E's* themes that the creator, Pixar's Andrew Stanton, is a Christian whose faith defined his approach to making the movie, especially in regard to the presentation of the dehumanizing effects of the attempt to create an earthly utopia (Megan Basham, "*Wall·E* World," *World,* June 28, 2008, http://www.worldmag.com/2008/06/walloe_world; Mark Moring, "The Little Robot that Could," *Christianity Today,* June 24, 2008, http://www.christianitytoday.com/ct/2008/juneweb-only/andrewstanton.html; "Christians in Cinema: Andrew Stanton," *ChristianCinema.com,* August 20, 2008, http://www.christiancinema.com/catalog/newsdesk_info.php?newsdesk_id=725).

broadest sense, including both nature and human nature.[2] Readers would do well, however, to watch this brilliant classic for themselves.

The first, most obvious theme of *Wall·E* is made depressingly clear from the opening scene. The little robot (named Wall·E) scoots around and patiently compacts mountains of trash in an environmentally destroyed and otherwise deserted planet. Earth is uninhabitable: the air and water are poisoned, all growing things have been destroyed, and the planet has turned into a dust-storm-racked desert with mountains of trash piled up amidst a desolated city landscape. The villain is not some evil mastermind, but a combination of human beings themselves, who have pursued the Baconian project of entirely mastering nature for the sake of this-worldly comfort and laborless ease, and the mega-corporation *Buy 'n' Large* that caters to and intensifies their consumerism.

From the decimated landscape of Earth, it's clear that neither the consumers nor the corporate purveyor of consumer goods cared about the effects of their feverish consumption on nature. The irony is that, since the project of mastery depends upon the passionate vexing of nature for the sake of this-worldly comfort, nature itself has been all but destroyed and human beings have been forced into space, there to inhabit an entirely artificial world on the giant *Buy 'n' Large* spaceship *Axiom*. Detached from nature, the people on *Axiom* become more and more dehumanized during their seven hundred year, multigenerational exile from Earth.

Most obviously, they become increasingly obese

---

[2] Importantly, the fictional utopia's aims in *Wall·E* fit snugly into Bacon's, an insight brilliantly argued by Sean Mattie in "*Wall·E* on the Problem of Technology," *Perspectives on Political Science*, 43 (2014): 12–20.

to the point where they are no longer able to walk (and so scoot around all day on robotic chairs). They are not connected to each other directly, but only through video screens continually projected in front of them. There are no meaningful goals to their existence or any higher aspects of human life that could pull their vision upward; they live merely to eat and zoom around the *Axiom's* mega-mall in their scooty chairs.

Each of these elements needs examination, not because our focus is an explication of *Wall·E*, but because what it portrays is a depressingly accurate satire of our way of life, beginning with the portrayal of Earth as a trashed planet.

This Land Is Your Land(fill)

It may seem, especially to those wary of environmentalists, that the movie's dismal opening scenes of Earth as a trash dump are just propaganda by extremists. As someone who has visited actual landfills, I beg to differ.

Before my first visit to a landfill, my family and I treated trash like everybody else. We put it into black plastic bags and then into the trash can for pickup. It went thereafter, so we supposed, to a magic, hidden destination where it disappeared for good. Out of sight, out of mind.

Things changed when, having moved out to rural southeastern Ohio, we tried to make a go of a more agrarian way of life, to which I would add my writing for financial support. This, I quickly found out, was not the way to become rich. We had to be very careful with our money, which fit well with my wife's frugal character.

Garbage collectors charge extra money for throwing away large items like rolls of old wire, hopelessly broken press-board furniture, dead appliances, and seedy couches. As a new denizen of rural life, I bought an old truck at auction—a *real* truck, a 1989 Ford F-150, not one of the newer, bulbous suburban pseudo-versions. So, we threw the junk in the bed of my beloved F-150, and off I went with my eldest son to the local landfill.

If you have never been to an actual landfill—never seen the acres and acres of ugly and malodorous detritus daily cast off by our consumerism, never smelled the suffocating rot in the air, never ridden across a quarter-mile road of smashed bottles, decaying food, soiled diapers, and shards of particle board to get to the designated dump site, never hastily unloaded your own contribution to the wasteland, and never run your eye down the endless line of railroad cars filled to overflowing and waiting to unload—you really should. You really, really should.

It was difficult enough having to take that first safari through a landfill, but I remember that we soon got another angle on trash. Sitting out behind our log cabin one day, we smelled a particularly nauseating odor bathing our bucolic back yard. It wasn't until a few weeks later that I discovered the source when I came upon a one-hundred-plus car railroad train that was parked on the tracks about a mile from our house. It was resting there while the other similarly-laden trains jostled for position to get into the landfill where I'd also dumped my own excess.

Then it hit me full-force. Those trains I'd previously seen at the landfill weren't from around *our* environs. As I found out, with a little research, Apex Landfill was shipping these tons and tons of trash in every day, train after train, hundreds and hundreds of cars from all over the eastern United States. We were privileged to enjoy the rotting of the Big Apple's garbage in our own backyard—

garbage that had disappeared like magic from NYC streets.

Garbage is big business, but it doesn't magically disappear. It's in someone else's back yard. I know. I've had it in mine. It is not rendered invisible. It is deeply repulsive, and makes one immediately ashamed of having thrown out so much crap.

Natural Waste and Unnatural Crap

Forgive my scatological language, but the word is entirely apropos, which is to say, biologically and ecologically accurate. All animals take in food and produce waste products. That is the way of life. For all other animals, the waste products are smaller than what they take in, and, even more ingenious, act as natural fertilizer for the ecosystem. Ingenious is the right word for the ecosystem in which animals live. To the mind unbiased by atheistic assumptions, Earth's ecosystem is a work of Genius in its complex, interconnected economy. Let's take a closer look.

Plants harvest energy from the Sun, taking in carbon dioxide and water, which allows them to produce their own carbon-based organic structures and to exhale oxygen as a waste product. In simplified chemical terms:

$$6CO_2 + 12H_2O \rightarrow [sunlight] \rightarrow C_6H_{12}O_6 + 6O_2 + 6H_2O.$$

Herbivorous animals eat plants and inhale oxygen, and as waste products emit carbon dioxide and water—these waste products being the very things that, in the cycle of life, plants take in. In simplified chemical terms:

$$C_6H_{12}O_6 + 6O_2 \rightarrow 6CO_2 + 6H_2O.$$

A wonderful cyclical design. One plant's trash (the waste product of photosynthesis, oxygen) is another animal's treasure (oxygen for respiration). One animal's trash (the waste product of respiration, carbon dioxide) is another plant's treasure (carbon dioxide for photosynthesis).

Obviously it's more complex than that. To add a bit more, plants eat sunlight, carbon dioxide, minerals from the ground, and water, turning the energy gained into living vegetable matter and giving off oxygen, both of which in turn fuel plant-eating, oxygen-breathing animals. These animals return carbon dioxide to the plants, along with manure, urine, and the natural fertilizer of their own rotting carcasses when they expire, and also provide more complex energy captured in the protein structure of their bodies for carnivorous animals. The carnivorous animals give back carbon dioxide, water, manure, and their rotting carcasses to the plants.

To repeat, a wonderful design, unmatched in its tightly-woven economy, and hence, the natural standard for ingenious efficiency.

And then there are human beings. By contrast, we human beings take in much, much more energy in carrying on our daily lives, and produce far, far more waste—very little of it performing the beneficial effects of fertilizer. The more "developed" we are, the greater the energy and materials we take in and the greater the waste we produce. I might illustrate this in quasi-chemical terms:

$$F_{ries} + C_{oke} + B_{urger} + D_{oritos} + DO_{nuts} + I_{phones} + N_{ew}Sn_{eakers} +$$
$$DE_{signer}Cl_{othes} + P_{lastic}H_2OBO_{ttles} + 6O_2 \rightarrow$$

$$G_{reasy}B_{ags} + Al_{cans} + G_{reasy}Wr_{apper} + F_{oil-lined}P_{lastic}B_{ags} + SO_{iled-}$$

$$P_{aper}BX + Ob_{solete}Ph_{one} + T_{orn}Ch_{eap}Sn_{eakers} + SoL_{ast}Ye_{ar}Cl_{othes} + Ug_{ly}Us_{eless}BO_{ttles} + 6\ CO_2 + 6H_2O.$$

Hence our crap. Mountains of it, albeit inverted mountains since we now dig gigantic holes in which to bury it.

You are well aware that I've included only the smallest fraction of what we take in on the left side of the human equation. It's an excellent exercise to list what we actually do take in on an average day to live as we in fact now live, and then, what we throw away because of it.

Not wanting to embarrass the reader, I'll do a rough inventory of my own energy and waste (in our household of five). First, the energy and materials input. I got up and made six cups of coffee. The coffee had to be grown elsewhere, processed and packaged, and shipped by truck to our grocery store. I ate some of my wife's homemade bread as toast, and added butter. The wheat, honey, salt, and yeast were produced elsewhere, packaged, and likewise shipped in; it took electricity to bake the bread, and a whole lot of energy and materials (steel, copper wire, plastic, computer chips, etc.) to make the oven, and the same is true of the toaster. I took a shower, using water that had to be purified at our local water plant—again, using a lot of machines and materials—and used soap and shampoo, manufactured, packaged, and shipped to our town. I got dressed in clothes, all of which (except underwear and socks) came from the thrift store, but even then, scads of materials were used in the original manufacturing. I drove my son to work, and then met my wife at morning Mass, and that involved a whole host of manufacturing to make all the multifarious car parts, extract and refine the petroleum into gasoline, and machines and materials to create and maintain the roads. When we came home, I had a banana, a cup of tea, and one of my wife's blueberry muffins, and then I came down to my basement office at 10:00 a.m. to write this paragraph on my computer (again, manufactured, packaged, and shipped, and now using electricity).

And now the waste. The waste that I produced so far in my own environs: coffee grounds, a used coffee filter; waste water from toilet, shower, and dishes; two Q-tips; a banana peel; a teabag; carbon dioxide, carbon monoxide, and nitrogen dioxide from my car. Not bad, until I take out the trash, and see two big empty chip bags, used paper towels, various glops of inedible plate-scrapings from last night's dinner, used cat litter, various jar lids and can tops, some grease, several gooped up plastic bags, and I don't want to dig down any further.

Don't forget the recycling, about four days' worth: four tuna cans, two mushroom cans, three tomato sauce cans, seven water bottles, five ginger ale cans, a cat litter container, two cat food cans, a lemon juice bottle, a salsa jar, the Sunday paper, the diocesan paper, several cardboard packages, a cardboard egg carton, and junk mail.

Then I recall all of the energy, machines, and materials (with all their attendant waste) it takes to provide us with electricity and water and the consequent waste this is continually producing.

And that's not all of it. We can't forget waste involved in the production of all the things I used, and each level of this production, packaging, and distribution it took to get it here. The amount of waste (largely hidden from us) that it takes to *produce* what we use dwarfs the amount of waste we generate from what we use. We in the United States produce more than 250 million tons of trash (or Municipal Solid Waste, MSW) per year, about the equivalent in

weight of almost 36 million African bull elephants, if you
need an odd but striking comparison. That's over four and
a half pounds per day per person. Even more revealing, it's
almost a 300 percent increase in MSW generation since
1960. Paper is the largest percentage in our garbage (about
33 percent), yard scraps and waste food count for about
12 percent each, and plastics for a little less, and the rest
is filled out with wood, cloth, rubber, leather, metal, glass,
and so on. The good news is that now over 30 percent of it
is recycled—paper and yard waste being the most recov-
erable, and (setting food aside) plastic the least—but still
over half goes to the landfill (the remaining percentage is
incinerated).[3]

But in order to produce the stuff that produced this
much waste, we generate "an additional 7.6 billion tons of
industrial waste, and 1.5 billion tons of mining waste, 3.2
billion tons of oil and gas, electric utility and cement kiln
wastes, and .5 billion tons of metal processing waste."[4]

So speaks the Law of Entropy. You can't get something
for nothing, and so the waste created in the production of
the empty plastic bottle you've just tossed, or the defunct
toaster, or the candy wrapper, far exceeds the bottle,
toaster, and wrapper themselves.

I am by no means innocent in this. In addition to all
I've noted above, I am also reminded of the broken washing
machine and two defunct driers in our garage, along with
one stinking microwave oven that I tried to fix (wasting

---

[3] See the most recent data in the Environmental Protection Agency's *Municipal Solid Waste Generation, Recycling, and Disposal in the United States:
Facts and Figures for 2007*, available at http://nepis.epa.gov/Exe/ZyPDF.
cgi/P1001UTO.PDF?Dockey=P1001UTO.PDF.

[4] Quoted in Elizabeth Royte, *Garbage Land: On the Secret Trail of Trash*
(New York: Little, Brown and Company, 2005), 238.

about thirty dollars and a lot of perspiration), a dead couch, a broken birdbath, two goner box springs and one mattress, one decrepit bicycle, a horrid particleboard computer table, a great pile of rotted wood pulled off of our deck, and several bags of whatnottery, all of which I was planning to take to the dump, but got so nauseated at the thought that I called someone else to do the dirty work.

Trickle-Down Trash

That's humbling. But something else is also maddening. All that crap at our local landfill? As I said, *most of it comes from elsewhere,* shipped in on trains, primarily from New York City. Why? For a long time NYC took care of its own garbage, and its notorious Fresh Kills landfill (opened in 1948) was the largest city landfill in the world. That makes statistical sense, since during the last half of the twentieth century, the US led the world in per capita energy consumption and garbage production, and NYC is our most populous city. But in 2001, tired of the ever-mounding nastiness on their own turf in Staten Island, NYC closed Fresh Kills, and started exporting its daily garbage to states in need of money who were willing (for economic reasons) to take millions upon millions of tons of other people's garbage. Our local landfill is smack in the middle of an economically depressed region of Ohio. Hence the endless trains full to overflowing with NYC's malodorous crap snaking through our local environs.[5]

That's a template of the flow of garbage worldwide: from richer, more developed areas that produce way more

---

[5] Ibid., 11, 53.

waste per capita but don't want it in their own backyard, to poorer areas that produce way less waste but need money so they accept the garbage of those who are better off. To be more brutally exact, the poor don't get the money (although some of it in the United States may indirectly benefit them through money paid for local enhancement projects, like parks or schools). But the bulk of the money goes to companies who locate the landfills in economically downtrodden areas.[6] Thanks, New York, New York.

While delivering a set of lectures in NYC a few years ago, I got a chance to see the fountainhead of all that garbage flowing into my home in rural rust-belt Ohio. I was staying a few blocks from the Empire State Building. What struck me (and unpleasantly so) when I looked out of my twenty-second-floor window was not only the famed city's general dirtiness and crampy smallness of the streets bearing an endless yellow flow of taxicabs, but the piles upon piles of bagged garbage that lined the streets every night awaiting the trucks that would magically spirit it all away, load it on rail cars, and send it on a one-way trip to dumpy, out-of-work, hickster, lowbrow Ohio so the high-brow, smugly self-righteous New Yorkers didn't have to see and acknowledge all the waste they produced.

Not that I'm bitter.

But here's what we all (especially you all in NYC) need to understand quite clearly. That waste doesn't just sit in a big pile underground in somebody else's back-yard. It leaches all kinds of wonderful nastiness into the ground, "battery acid, nail polish remover, pesticides, and paint, combined with liquid versions of rotting food, pet feces, medical waste, and diapers," and you can fill out the

---

6   Ibid., 40–42, 153.

list. As water runs through it, landfills produce a leachate filled with toxins such as "oil and grease, cyanide, arsenic, cadmium, chromium, copper, lead, nickel, silver, mercury, and zinc."[7]

Attempts have been made to seal off landfills completely, creating so-called dry landfills, but the result is both unhelpful and unsavory: nothing rots, so that you end up with the now famous forty-year-old un-decomposed hot dog that garbage "archaeologists" unearthed.[8] Going away from dry landfills, newer landfills allow for decomposition, treating the leachate and trapping the methane released by rotting (rather than letting it explode, or burn underground for years). But even the best landfills will let more and more toxic leachate leak out as the landfill ages, and trap at most 75 percent of the greenhouse gas methane.[9]

I've left unmentioned the waste we produce that is the most obvious indicator of the level of our development: electronic waste, or, e-waste. Isn't it grand that we have nice, slim TV and computer screens now? That our personal computers are ever thinner, faster, and more powerful than all the ones we used to own (for me, going back to that lovely glowing computer troglodyte, a Kaypro)? That our old clunky shoe-sized cell phones have been replaced by sleeker, more technologically advanced models—and we can trade up every year? Where did all the old electronic stuff go? Did it magically disappear? It went into the landfill. (Although some of it is recycled, a point we'll pick up on below.)

Developed nations like the United States produce

---

[7] Ibid., 58.

[8] Ibid., 89.

[9] Ibid., 92–93.

the most garbage, and living near a landfill daily replen-
ished by someone else's trash can indeed make one bitter.
But people that live near landfills in undeveloped countries suffer a far worse indignity than I ever have: these
poorest of the poor don't just live near landfills, they live
right *next to* landfills, so they can sort through the newly
unloaded garbage for food and any salvageable items to
sell or recycle. Witness the Dandora dump in Nairobi,
Kenya.[10] Or the Payatas dump outside of Quezon City in
the Philippines.[11]

The Poor Recycling

And don't think that there's a simple, morally unambiguous solution to all this crap: just recycle it! I'm all for
recycling, but it's not the silver bullet solution. To begin
with, it smacks of the "out of sight, out of mind" mentality.
We happily put our plastic and glass bottles, our alumini-
um cans, our paper, and so on, in our nice blue boxes, and
believe that it's all magically transformed again into wonderful goods, either by machines or happy elves. The truth
is that what makes recycling economically feasible is that
very poor people in other countries (mostly China)—who
get very little money—can sort through it by hand, and do
so in exceedingly unhealthy conditions, and then reclaim
it using processes that are highly polluting (because

---

[10] See "Toxic Kenya dump embodies Pope Francis' environmental concerns,"
    USA Today, November 24, 2015, http://www.usatoday.com/story/news/
    world/2015/11/24/toxic-kenya-dump-embodies-pope-francis-environ-
    mental-concerns/76329668/.

[11] See a trailer for a documentary on the Payatas dump at http://mirage-
    pro.net/payatasclip.html.

there are so few, if any, restrictions on industrial waste in China—or India or Africa, for that matter). As recycling expert Adam Minter says, "the hand labor of Chinese workers is essential to recycling the wasted luxuries of American and other developed world consumers."[12] Ditto Africa and India.[13]

So, we ship our old televisions, computers, telephones, and other decrepit or merely slightly-out-of-date electronics to China, and peasants take them apart, piece by piece, burn the plastic off the metal wires or the circuit board, inhaling the leaded fumes that arise so they can get to the precious metal. This aspect of recycling isn't very romantic, releasing, as it does, clouds of poison into the peasants' lungs and into their environs.[14]

If you think recycling is pretty on the other end, go to the notorious recycling center in Guiyu, China, the biggest electronics recycling location in the world. Over 80 percent of the children suffer from lead poisoning, 25 percent of newborns have elevated levels of the toxin cadmium, and the water and air are hyper-polluted.[15] The poor don't worry about the health effects, because the little money they get for exposing themselves to unregulated reclamation of the metals keeps them from starving now.[16] That's what makes recycling pay.

---

[12] Adam Minter, *Junkyard Planet: Travels in the Billion-Dollar Trash Trade* (New York: Bloomsbury, 2013), 71. This is a more popular account of the good and bad entailed in recycling. For a more thorough, scholarly account, including what may be done, see Samantha MacBride, *Recycling Reconsidered: The Present Failure and Future Promise of Environmental Action in the United States* (Cambridge, MA: MIT Press, 2012).

[13] Ibid., 98–101.

[14] Ibid., 65–66, 75, 140.

[15] Ibid., 185.

[16] Ibid., 193.

And it pays in strange ways. The peasants in Guiyu, working in horrid conditions, sort through old electronics by hand, extracting processing parts which will then be sold to China's toy manufacturers—you know, the ones that make all the Christmas toys that you flip upside down and the label declares, "Made in China," which is to say, almost any toy you buy. "Think about that," Minter says, "somewhere, a parent is giving a child a toy made from used computer chips extracted in one of Guiyu's notorious workshops."[17]

How about all those plastic bottles? They're not shipped to recycling elves either. They're shipped to China in enormous bales. "China is the world's largest scrap-plastics importer and processor," and Wen'an County in China "is at the heart of the global scrap-plastic trade." What is most striking about Wen'an, reports Minter, is that "there's nothing green. It's a dead zone. . . . It wasn't always this way."

> Twenty-five years ago, Wen'an was bucolic—an agricultural region renowned for its streams, peach trees, and simple, rolling landscape. The people who knew it then sigh when they recall the fragrant soil, the fishing, and the soft summer nights. Engage a local in conversation, and within minutes you'll hear how you should've come in the old days, back before the business of Wen'an was the business of recycling (plastic) automobile bumpers, plastic bags, and bleach containers, back when the frogs and crickets were so loud they drowned out human conversation, back before the plastics' re-

---

[17] Ibid., 201.

cycling trade plasticized the lungs of men in their twenties, way before multinational companies did business in Wen'an so they could say their products were "made from recycled plastics."[18]

Notes Minter, "Wen'an is the most polluted place I've ever visited. . . . the scale of the pollution, covering much of the county's 450 square miles, is unmatched anywhere else I've been, in any other country on earth."[19]

It's not difficult to understand why, and what the toll on those living there means. "Environmental and safety equipment is neither required nor available . . ." and it wouldn't be used anyway, because then it wouldn't pay them in Wen'an to recycle our plastic.[20] Employees of recyclers there are "scrawny and bug-eyed," wear no protective clothing, sort through our trash, shred it, and clean it in tubs filled with caustic cleaning fluid (fumes rising into their unprotected lungs), get what they can, and throw the waste products of recycling—unsalvageable plastic bits and cleaning chemicals—into an open pit at the edge of town.[21] Needless to say, the "industry" makes the people sick: people in their late twenties develop pulmonary fibrosis and experience paralyzing strokes, among their various ills.[22] That's the real face of much of our plastic recycling.

If all our recycling were done here, in America, where it's generated, *and* we paid American wages to the workers, *and* reclamation was done under our far stricter

---

[18] Ibid., 146.

[19] Ibid., 155.

[20] Ibid., 148.

[21] Ibid., 150–151. The entirety of chapter 9 must be read to take in the full foulness of plastic recycling.

[22] Ibid., 157.

environmental standards—there would be no recycling. It would be far, far too expensive. Factories in America devoted to reclaiming scrap copper "shut down in 2000 due to the high cost of complying with environmental regulations. . . . Partly as a result, China, which barely had a copper refining business in 1980, now has the world's largest." Again, it's not just the lack of environmental standards in China. "It's too expensive to recycle without cheap labor to extract the metal."[23] *That* is what our recycling efforts depend upon.

And it's not just the cheap labor or lack of worker protection and environmental regulations we should worry about. It's the fact that we don't actually produce all the stuff we consume: China does. Recycling pays, in great part, because the enormous ships China sends over with nearly all the manufactured products we consume would go back to China entirely empty—since we have nothing to sell them—if it weren't for our scrap paper, plastic containers, cans, old electronics, and engines. Empty ships don't earn money, and our crap provides ballast as well.[24] That makes it cheaper to ship to China, than it is, say, halfway across the country. For example, it would be four times more expensive to ship the same amount from Los Angeles to Chicago as it would from Los Angeles to China.[25]

A further reason our recycling pays is that China, which is quickly catching up with us in its own hyper-consumption, desperately needs the recycled raw materials.[26] In other words, if we two giants didn't frantically consume,

---

[23] Ibid., 117–118.

[24] Ibid., chap. 5.

[25] Ibid., 87.

[26] Ibid., 94–95.

recycling wouldn't pay, and therefore it wouldn't happen. When the 2008 housing industry crash occurred, through the collusion of banksters and foolish and/or corrupt politicians, the market for recycled materials crashed with it because manufacturing all but halted.[27] And what happened on our end when China suddenly stopped buying our recycling in the 2008 crash? We just threw it all in the landfill—paper, plastic, cans, metal scrap—all of it.[28]

Flushed with Unsuccess

That brings us back full circle, back home from China, to our own mountains of waste. But I should note that landfills aren't the only waste problem. I've yet to mention the other kind that found its way out of NYC to rural Ohio: sewer sludge. It's just exactly what you think it is. NYC's treated sewage waste—the solid stuff, left over after processing at the sewage treatment plant—is turned into fertilizer, labeled with the more elegant name "biosolids," and shipped to rural areas where it is given away as free fertilizer to farmers (or even better, farmers are paid to allow it to be spread on their fields).

Did I *read* about this? No, I didn't have to do research into the facts; the facts came to us. One day, a really, really awful smell came creeping down into the hollow in which our aforementioned rural cabin was located. It was so bad, so acrid, that you wanted to shake your head and spit. We had no idea what it was until one of our neighbors, a man named Custer, came torching down the hill in his truck

<hr />

[27] Ibid., 132.
[28] Ibid., 236.

a day or two after, pulled into our driveway, and started releasing an equally toxic stream of expletives. (Not that his speech was altogether pure on a good day, which is why we nicknamed him General Cusser.) But he had especial eloquence on that day, lathering his profanities with obscenities, which, when we picked through the actual words for the few that were substantive and repeatable, revealed to us the cause of the Big Stink. A farmer just down the road had agreed to spread "biosolids" on his corn and soybean fields as, not just free, but we'll-pay-you-to-take-it fertilizer. General Cusser just had his well tested and found things one does not want to drink. He was ready to take justice into his own hands (with the help of good neighbors, such as yours truly).

Happily, the local uproar led by Custer's charge was such that the farmer ceased delivery. Good thing because the reported ill effects of longer term exposure aren't pleasant on people in the environs of sludge-cum-fertilizer dumpings: "abscesses, reproductive complications, cysts, tumors, asthma, skin lesions, gastrointestinal problems, headaches, nosebleeds, and irritation of the skin and respiratory tract," and death (of livestock and people).[29]

The problem with sewer sludge is that it's not actually fertilizer, even though the EPA allows the misleading label. It's toxic. That's why no one wants it. New York City used to dump its sludge ten miles offshore, but it killed the fish in the dump area. Then it shipped it on sludge tankers over a hundred miles away, but soon fishermen noticed that it made the fish sick.

What to do? The Environmental Protection Agency helped out in 1993 by raising the acceptable limits of

---

[29] Royte, 222–223.

toxins so that what was once labeled "hazardous waste," could be packaged as fertilizer. Today, half of our country's sludge is thus repackaged. NYC used to ship it out to Colorado, until the folks on the receiving end tired of its malodorous consequences. It's now spread on Ohio fields and Florida orange groves. The exciting thing, as *Garbage Land*'s author Elizabeth Royte points out, is that "sludge sold as fertilizer can be so contaminated with toxins that it can't legally, under the EPA's Part 503 rules [governing sludge], be buried in landfills designed for household waste."[30] If something smells morally funny here, that's because, as Royte adds, "the scientific studies on which the agency based its original sludge regulations were performed by the sludge industry itself."[31]

Back to the Left and Right

Now at this point I'd like us to pause and go back to our slight overgeneralizations about Left and Right. I don't think I need to convince anyone on the Left that all this waste generation stinks, that it's dead-ugly, and that it allows for an ever-spreading degradation of our environment due to conspicuous overconsumption. And I especially wouldn't need to convince them that "out of sight, out of mind" is a morally malodorous way to deal with the entire waste generation problem. Nor would I have any difficulty in persuading them that we've got to do something, and quickly. The Left gets it—thankfully.

    I do admit to enjoying the tweaking of folks from New

---

[30] Ibid., 216. On sewer sludge, see chapter 11.
[31] Ibid., 223.

York City, who generally lean far to the self-righteous Left, and who believe that planting herbs in window boxes, drinking Fair Trade coffee, and recycling fruit-scented water bottles exonerates them from creating so much trash and dumping it on other people. The Big Appleans believe they are the country's physicians, but really ought to spend some time healing themselves.

The Right? That's another story, or better, it will take another angle. Let's start this way. All you folks on the Right, who are generally Christians but who don't think our ever-mounting mountains of trash are a problem, climb in your SUV and betake yourself out to the nearest landfill. Get out and take a deep breath, and recite the following verses from Genesis.

And God said, "Let the waters under the heavens be gathered together into one place, and let the dry land appear." And it was so. God called the dry land Earth, and the waters that were gathered together he called Seas. And God saw that it was good. . . .

And God said, "Let the earth bring forth living creatures according to their kinds: cattle and creeping things and beasts of the earth according to their kinds." And it was so. And God made the beasts of the earth according to their kinds and the cattle according to their kinds, and everything that creeps upon the ground according to its kind. And God saw that it was good.

Then God said, "Let us make man in our image, after our likeness; and let them have dominion over the fish of the sea, and over the birds of the air, and over the cattle, and over all the earth, and over every creeping thing that creeps upon the earth." So God created man in his own image, in the image of God he created him; male and female he created them. And God blessed them, and God said to them, "Be fruitful and multiply, and fill the earth and subdue it; and have dominion over the fish of the sea and over the birds of the air and over every living thing that moves upon the earth." And God said, "Behold, I have given you every plant yielding seed which is upon the face of all the earth, and every tree with seed in its fruit; you shall have them for food. And to every beast of the earth, and to every bird of the air, and to everything that creeps on the earth, everything that has the breath of life, I have given every green plant for food." And it was so. And God saw everything that he had made, and behold, it was very good. And there was evening and there was morning, a sixth day. (Gen 1:9–10, 24–31)

Now take a good look at that landfill. See all that you have made. Do you call it very good? Is this what our rule over the earth was supposed to look like? Is that how you express gratitude to your Creator?

How about reciting a few Psalms? Let's try Psalm 8:

O LORD, our Lord,
how majestic is your name in all the earth!
You whose glory above the heavens is chanted
by the mouth of babes and infants,
you have founded a bulwark because of your foes,
to still the enemy and the avenger.
When I look at thy heavens, the work of your fingers,

the moon and the stars which you have
     established;
what is man that you are mindful of him,
and the son of man that you care for him?
Yet you have made him little less than the angels,
and you have crowned him with glory and honor.
You have given him dominion over the works of
     your hands;
you have put all things under his feet,
all sheep and oxen,
and also the beasts of the field,
the birds of the air, and the fish of the sea,
whatever passes along the paths of the sea.
O LORD, our Lord,
how majestic is your name in all the earth!

Do these words of praise for the God of creation stick in your craw? Is this steaming pile of toxic filth in front of you the result of our rule over the work of the Lord's hands? Is this "everything" what should be "under our feet"? Does this vile landscape make one want to sing of the majesty of God over all the earth?

Psalm 24:1 anyone: "The earth is the LORD'S, and the fulness thereof"? Really?

Or Psalm 104:24: "O LORD, how manifold are your works! In wisdom you have made them all; . . . May the glory of the LORD endure for ever; may the LORD rejoice in his works . . ." Does He rejoice in *that*?

And if that doesn't wake you up, how about a little from Romans 1: "Ever since the creation of the world his invisible nature, namely, his eternal power and deity, has been clearly perceived in the things that have been made" (v. 24).

Well, if God's creation was designed, in its order and beauty, to shine forth as undeniable truth of His existence, wisdom, and goodness, what does this giant man-made blight do? If we, who are supposedly made in the image of God, so befoul the gift of creation made by God to proclaim the Creator's glory, small wonder that the atheists and secular-minded on the Left are disinclined to consider the merits of our belief in God, but instead, turn away from Christians as hypocrites.

And finally, there's this passage from the Gospel of John, which should make us drop to our knees: "In the beginning was the Word, and the Word was with God, and the Word was God. He was in the beginning with God; all things were made through him, and without him was not anything made that was made" (Jn 1:1). What have we done to what was made through Him? Look out on this ruined landscape. If you were the avowed enemy of the Creator, what more could you do to profane His handiwork, this beloved Earth made by God with human beings at its pinnacle?

If we really believe that nature is created by God, and that nature is good and manifests God's wisdom in its beauty, order, and wisdom, then why are those on the Left, who are generally religiously disinclined, far more appreciative and protective of the beauty, order, and wisdom of nature than we Christians are?

"The earth, our home, is beginning to look more and more like an immense pile of filth. In many parts of the planet . . . once beautiful landscapes are now covered with rubbish." So spoke Pope Francis in his encyclical *Laudato si'*.[32]

---

[32] *Laudato si'*, §21.

Get one more good look at the landfill. Just because you don't happen to see this immense pile of filth in your own neighborhood, doesn't mean you and I aren't responsible for it.

But now we need to add something—something that will make both the Left and Right uncomfortable. The mountain of foulness spread out in front of you is as large as it is because of *sin*, in fact, more than one: the sin of greed (or avarice) and the sin of gluttony (both of which violate the virtue of temperance). These are two of the Seven Deadly Sins, ranked from the worst to least bad: Pride, Envy, Wrath, Sloth, Greed, Gluttony, and Lust. If we really thought about the causes of all the garbage more carefully, we could easily make a case for Envy and Lust, and perhaps Sloth, contributing multiple layers to the dump as well: envy at the goods of others, so we buy more than we need; lust, insofar as sex is used to sell and oversell nearly everything these days; and sloth, insofar as we are so wedded to convenience that we consider any effort on our part to reduce our trash production to be an insufferable burden.

But bringing in the Deadly Sins makes the Left nervous because, generally having cheerfully embraced secularism, it has had to give up the benefit of being able to call something a sin and mean it. Sin is a fundamental hell-worthy violation of our nature, a destruction of the virtues that we must have to be good human beings, and most important, an affront to the Creator God who made us. Its very badness consists in its destruction of goodness. But it's difficult to say that something is a sin if there's no God.

Furthermore, if there is no God, then some people may really happen to care if we're making great piles of trash and sacking the environment, but others may simply give a shrug and say, "So what? I'll be dead in another twenty-five years, and it's not in my backyard. And frankly, I don't care anyway. You only live once."

This "So what?" response is, in fact, rooted in the original atheism of Machiavelli, which in denying the existence of God and the soul also denied that there was any real distinction between good and evil. Good was getting what you want in this life, no matter what it took. So, "Eat junk food, drink soda, and be merry, and don't bother recycling, for tomorrow we shall die! We have no souls. We are only bodies. The pleasures of the body are our only real goods, so we'd better get all we can in the only life we have. Trash up the earth because there ain't no heaven."

And that leads us to another surprising point for the Left to consider. The reason that we human beings are able to create so much trash is that we are *not* just another animal. We are (as the ancients rightly called us) the only *rational* animal, a creature that has intellectual capabilities so far above any other animal on the earth that we seem to be gods by comparison. This capacity makes us godlike in more than one way: we have astounding intellectual capacities, and the free will to use them, and from these also come equally profound moral capacities. We are the only animal given the gift of reason. With this gift, our choices as human beings—good and bad—are magnified exponentially.

No other animal has uncovered the mystery of electricity or unwound the secrets of DNA or figured out plate tectonics or split the atom or deciphered the chemical elements on the Periodic Table. No other animal has to make decisions about what to do with such knowledge, and so no other animal can be held morally responsible for making evil choices. And evil choices don't just mean blowing up the world or Frankenstein-fiddling with the DNA of plants, animals, and human beings. It also means creating ever-higher piles of toxic garbage as the waste product of our self-indulgence.

So, you on the Left, who like to portray human beings as a nothing-special animal, an accidentally produced variant ape: you have to admit that human beings are, by comparison, so far above other animals in their capacities that a merely accidental universe could not have contrived them. If you don't want to admit that, then you'll have trouble explaining the immense scientific-technological capacities that went into creating all this crap in the landfills, since no other animal could possibly do it, and even more, you'll have trouble holding human beings *morally* accountable for the mess. Do you hold any other animal morally accountable for anything? Why single out *this* generally hairless biped for moral censure?

But this should all make the Right nervous as well, since it generally upholds belief in God as essential to the moral order designed by the Creator. We couldn't generate this much trash without engaging in full-steam intemperance (the vice opposed to the virtue of temperance), without indulging ourselves unnecessarily, without eating way too much, without buying way too much, and without some people making huge profits on other people's lack of self-control. You can't believe that God and sin are real and deny the fact that Gluttony and Greed are real sins, and you can't believe that Gluttony and Greed are real sins and not see the vast wasteland of waste as a visible representation of the invisible damage caused to the souls of those who either suffer or profit from such indulgence.

And that brings up an interesting point for everyone, but especially for Christians: sin damages the soul, even if we could remove the external effects. So, even if we recycled 100 percent of our waste without creating any waste or treating human beings like throwaway slaves, and there were no mountains of trash blighting the landscape and poisoning the ground water, we would still be corrupting our souls by the vice of intemperance. Sin is sin, whether we remove the visible effects from our field of vision, or (we should add) whether it leads to greater economic prosperity.

So both sides have something to think about, but we're not going to let it end at just these initial reflections on ecology. We need to see far more deeply how interconnected true ecology really is, how the natural order, especially as it includes us human beings, necessarily has essentially theological, social, economic, and moral dimensions that will surprise and enlighten both the Left and Right, and reveal a truly catholic ecology.

CHAPTER FOUR

Dehumanization and Food Pollution

Wall·E *and Obesity*

Back to *Wall·E* again. What about those human beings who, after sacking the earth with trash, fouling its air, and poisoning its water, are swirling around space for seven hundred years? As the movie presents it, the salvaged human race has quite literally forgotten Earth and lives instead in the entirely artificial world inside the spaceship *Axiom*. Since technology has entirely mastered nature, the men and women have nothing to do but zip around all day in a giant shopping mall on self-propelled comfy chairs, talking to each other on computer screens projected in front of their faces, eating snack food delivered by robots, playing video golf, and gossiping.

The movie brilliantly portrays the dehumanizing effects of their entirely artificial life devoted to comfort and pleasure. Being entirely sedentary, they physically balloon, becoming so obese that they cannot walk and their feet have therefore become pudgy vestigial organs. Gender has been all but erased because males and females have become almost indistinguishable blobs. Both sexes are bored because they have no meaningful goal in their shallow lives other than the endless pursuit of their own physical comfort. There is no romance. The natural effect of romance, babies, has another cause. They are somehow artificially produced on board the spaceship. There are no marriages and no families. As noted, the grown-ups talk to one another only through screens (even when they are zipping around *Axiom's* megamall side by side). The endless mounds of trash created on the ship are continually gathered by robots, compacted, and shot out into space. Out in space, out of mind.

This is obviously a satire, a prophetic window opened up so that we can look to our future, the future of nature fully conquered for our comfort. It's a world where we human beings don't work because robots do. A world where we not only don't walk but increasingly can't walk. A world where screens have replaced face-to-face conversations. A world where the pursuit of comfort has led to a shallow consumerist existence. A world where we're so out of shape that we've taken on another shape.

A world that sounds a bit too familiar.

The folks producing *Wall·E* could have been even harder on us, but since it's a kid's movie, they couldn't portray some of the darker aspects of the Baconian pursuit of physical gratification as enhanced by screen technology—aspects we're already experiencing, such as porn addiction, sexting between kids, and solitary sex enhanced by robotics (not the cute ones in *Wall·E*, but sexbots designed as mechanical sex slaves).

We'll consider pornography as a kind of moral pollution in the next chapter. In this chapter, we're dealing with another kind of moral pollution, which we might call "food pollution." But first, we need a larger account of human moral nature through which we can understand both kinds of pollution.

Moral Pollution vs. Moral Health, Vice vs. Virtue

The pursuit of physical comfort and convenience that produces the external effect of so many mountains of trash also produces human beings entirely absorbed in technologically-enhanced sensual pleasures, an absorption that fundamentally dehumanizes them. One form of dehumanization is obesity.

Why am I counting obesity as a form of *moral* pollution? Because it is the result of denying the essential human importance of the moral virtue of temperance, one of the four Cardinal Virtues (the other three being prudence, justice, and courage).

What is temperance? We might do better to begin with the more fundamental question, what is a virtue? As ancient ethicists well understood, human beings are essentially moral creatures; that is, unlike other animals that are largely governed by instinct, human beings have to *choose* to do the things that are actually good for their particular nature.

In the wild—away from human beings and their dumpsters and garbage cans—animals eat what is actually good for them according to their particular bodily constitutions. As a consequence, there are no obese animals in the wild. But because we human beings are *rational* animals, we need to think about, produce, and choose what to eat. We aren't automatically led to what is healthy; in fact, it is precisely because of our rationality and free will that we can choose to invent and eat snack food rather than to eat naturally healthy food. We can choose badly, and make a habit of it, thereby harming or even destroying our health.

The habit of choosing well in regard to food is a particu-

lar kind of *virtue*, virtue being the habit-formed power to
choose the right thing. This particular virtue dealing with
food is fairly close to the modern understanding of, say,
having good eating habits, which are only gotten through
repeatedly eating the right foods. Such good eating habits
define one's tastes, so that the food that is actually healthy
for us pleases us as well. When we habitually eat good
things, we have the particular virtue of *temperance* (at least
in regard to food). But we can also have bad eating habits.
The habit of eating unhealthy things is one manifestation
of the vice of *intemperance*.

This is not some kind of modern discovery. "Temperance is . . . concerned with pleasures," we are told by the
ancient Greek philosopher Aristotle. But not all pleasures;
rather, only particular pleasures of the body: "Pleasures
that concern temperance and intemperance are those that
are shared with the other animals. . . . These pleasures are
touch and taste," that is, the pleasures of sex and eating.[1]

The pleasures of sex and eating we share with the
other animals. In all animals (including us) they are obviously for the sake of making more animals and for taking
in food to stay alive. But again, we are a very different
kind of animal. We rational animals—we human beings—
are the only animals capable of detaching the pleasures
of sex from procreation and the pleasure of eating from
its proper nutritional goal. For Aristotle, that detachment
and subsequent focus on pleasure alone as the highest
good is a vice: intemperance. The intemperate person is a
slave to the pleasures he or she pursues, whether it's junk
food or junk sex.

---

[1] Aristotle, *Nicomachean Ethics*, trans. Terence Irwin (Indianapolis, IN:
    Hackett, 1985), 1117b23–1119b20.

Or, to get another account, we might use the *Catechism of the Catholic Church* as a witness. "*Temperance* is the moral virtue that moderates the attraction of pleasures and provides balance in the use of created goods" (CCC 1809). The virtue of temperance ensures that we are not slaves to our appetites, either for food or sex, but direct them to our proper, natural good. The Catechism adds that this is part of our *moral* responsibility to use the good things given to us by the Creator well, neither overindulging in them or wasting them. That would be a sin. Sins dehumanize because they turn us into pleasure-obsessed, self-destructive animals rather than creatures made in the image of God.

Necessary and Instructive Provisos

Before I raise too many hackles here, I realize that the causes of obesity are complex, even while the effect is the same: harming the health of the human body and the lack of the ability not to eat to excess. We know, for example, that morbid or severe adult obesity is sometimes associated with childhood sexual and physical abuse.[2] But

---

[2]   A. S. Richardson, W. H. Dietz, and P. Gordon-Larsen, "The association between childhood sexual and physical abuse with incident adult severe obesity across 13 years of the National Longitudinal Study of Adolescent Health," *Pediatric Obesity* 9 (2014): 351–361; Helen Smith, et al., "Sexual Abuse, Sexual Orientation, and Obesity in Women," *Journal of Women's Health* 19, no. 8 (2010): 1525–1532; E. Hemmingsson, K. Johansson, and S. Reynisdottir, "Effects of childhood abuse on adult obesity: a systematic review and meta-analysis," *World Obesity Reviews* 15 (2014): 882–893; Orit Pinhas-Hamiel, D. Modan-Moses, M. Herman-Raz, and B. Reichman, "Obesity in girls and penetrative sexual abuse in childhood," *Acta Pædiatrica* 98 (2009): 144–147.

this brings us back to the need for other virtues, making evident the danger entailed in the lack of the virtues of sexual temperance and gentleness (the virtue that deals with moderating anger) of the abusers.

There is also a significant "comorbid" connection between depression and obesity, although it is unclear which may be the cause and which the effect in particular instances, and the causes of depression are myriad.[3] For example, as we'll see in the next chapter, pornography is now a leading cause of marital destruction, and the emotional damage to women is often handled by turning to comfort food.[4] Again, we find ourselves confronting the effect of a sexual vice (intemperance in regard to sexual desire) on the ability to have and sustain a moral virtue (temperance in regard to food).

And we cannot fail to mention what should be the obvious contributing cause to the epidemic of obesity in our contemporary culture: the dual, related rise of televisions, computers, video games, smartphones, *and* a sedentary lifestyle and economy based upon them. We don't move; we eat junk food while we don't move; we become obese. This brings in a more complex set of cultural-technological causes, which give us a needed expansion of our notion of human ecology, one which includes fundamental questions about both economics and technology. We'll be attending to these things as well in this and the rest of the chapters, where we'll see why economics and technology must be considered part of our moral ecology.

---

[3] K. Preiss, L. Brennan, and D. Clarke, "A systematic review of variables associated with the relationship between obesity and depression," *Obesity Reviews* 14 (2013): 906–918.

[4] See Mary Eberstadt's *Adam and Eve after the Pill: Paradoxes of the Sexual Revolution* (San Francisco: Ignatius, 2012), 51.

But whatever the causes, the *effect* is the same: harmful obesity brought about by the consumption of too much food, especially high-calorie, highly-processed, low-nutrition junk food, and that consumption involves, one way or another, the loss of or lack of the virtue of temperance. Like it or not, we have to deal with obesity because obesity over the last few decades has quite literally become an epidemic.

The Obesity Epidemic

Note an important thing about our dealings with food: in regard to the virtue of temperance, the moral standard is not arbitrary but defined by the health of the human body itself. It's not a matter of opinion whether pounding down cola, chips, and candy are good for us any more than it's a matter of opinion whether dumping toxic chemicals into massive landfills is good for the environment. Like the natural order, the human body has an intrinsic natural, physiological order, independent of anyone's opinion about it, that defines what is good for it. When we choose badly in regard to that intrinsic natural bodily order—that is, when we eat piles of junk food—we only harm our own health. Obesity is one result among many, including heart disease, diabetes, osteoporosis, high blood pressure, and so on.

Obesity through intemperance is a worldwide, growing problem, especially in the English-speaking, high-income, more industrialized regions, as the most recent study has shown.[5] Much to our shame, the US ranks

---

[5] See Majid Ezzati, et al., "Trends in adult body-mass index in 200 countries from 1975 to 2014: a pooled analysis of 1698 population-based

number one: it had the greatest number of *severely* obese men and women during the entire study years, stretching from 1975 to 2014. The number of severely obese men in the US rose from 1.1 million to 16.2 million during this period, and severely obese women from 3 million to 23.1 million. China, with its hyper-industrialization during this period, jetted up from sixtieth to second (males) and forty-first to second (females) during the same period.[6] Moreover, "Obesity rates are especially troubling in children, rising at three times the rate of increase in adults," as other recent research reveals.[7] Experts Kelly D. Brownell (Yale) and Kenneth E. Warner (University of Michigan) add the unpleasant but telling fact, "Indeed, the term adult

---

measurement studies with 19.2 million participants," *Lancet* 387 (2016): 1377–1396. The analysis was done not merely by weight, but by Body-Mass Index (in terms of kilograms per square meter, kg/m^2), measuring the increase, worldwide, from 1975–2014. The results are unpleasant.

Global age-standardised mean BMI in men increased from 21.7 kg/m^2 . . . in 1975 to 24·2 kg/m^2 . . . in 2014, and in women from 22.1 kg/m^2 . . . in 1975 to 24.4 kg/m^2 . . . in 2014. . . . The largest increase in men's mean BMI occurred in high-income English-speaking countries (1.00 kg/m^2 per decade; . . . and in women in central Latin America (1.27 kg/m^2 per decade . . .). The increase in women's mean BMI was also more than 1.00 kg/m^2 per decade in Melanesia, Polynesia and Micronesia, high-income English-speaking countries, southeast Asia, Andean Latin America, and the Caribbean. Because of these trends, men and women in high-income English-speaking countries in 2014 had substantially higher BMIs than those in continental Europe, whereas in 1975 their BMI had been similar or lower, especially for women. . . . By contrast with these large increases, the rise in women's mean BMI was less than 0.2 kg/m^2 per decade in central Europe, southwestern Europe, and high-income Asia Pacific.

6   Ibid., 1388.
7   Kelly D. Brownell and Kenneth E. Warner, "The Perils of Ignoring History: Big Tobacco Played Dirty and Millions Died. How Similar Is Big Food?" *The Milbank Quarterly* 87, no. 1 (2009): 259–294.

onset diabetes has now been scrapped and replaced with Type 2 diabetes because children as young as eight are developing the disease."[8] If that weren't awful enough for children, the rise in maternal obesity is not only bad for the mothers, but causes significant health problems for babies in the womb.[9]

As former Food and Drug Administration commissioner David Kessler, M.D., has noted, this trend marks a significant kind of human watershed in our history. This many human beings have never been this fat, and here we don't just mean the sheer numbers, but the percentage of the population, and America is leading that trend.[10] It isn't in our genes. We can't blame it on our metabolism. It's a *cultural* problem that has arisen fairly recently in human history.

A Painful Thought Experiment for Lent

But we need to broaden our understanding of the full effect of *cultural* intemperance to include economic and environmental considerations. In the spring semester, depending upon what I'm teaching, I'll often have my students engage in a thought experiment at the beginning of Lent (the Catholic season of forty days of fasting leading up to Easter). Of course, like me, they are all giving up a little something—sweets, donuts, sugar in their coffee—or,

---

[8] Ibid., 262.

[9] Meaghan A. Leddy, Michael L. Power, and Jay Schulkin, "The Impact of Maternal Obesity on Maternal and Fetal Health," *Reviews In Obstetrics & Gynecology* 1, no. 4 (2008): 170–178.

[10] David A. Kessler, *The End of Overeating: Taking Control of the Insatiable American Appetite* (New York: Rodale, 2009), chap. 1.

for the really brave, coffee itself. "What would happen," I ask, "if for the forty days of Lent all Christians in America gave up all foods except exactly what their bodies actually need for health?" That's somewhere around 230,000,000 people suddenly eating only for the sake of their real nutritional needs.

Usually they choose the most obvious results: "We'd all be a lot healthier." "People would lose weight." "We'd have developed entirely new, healthy eating habits."

All true. I would lose much of my extra twenty-five pounds. But then I push them: What about the *economic* consequences? What would happen to McDonald's, Burger King, and all the other fast-food companies—not just the CEOs, but all the employees? Or think on this: go to your local convenience store and grocery store, and see how much of what they sell is hyper-processed convenience or junk food. What would happen to all those jobs connected to all this unhealthy junk—not just folks in the companies that produce the Coke, Tater Tots, and chips themselves, but those who make all the packaging, the guys who deliver all this stuff to the stores, the people paid to market it, the machines used in the manufacturing, and all the extra employees in the store where it's sold?

The answer is rather startling. Lent is six weeks, an economically significant chunk of time. On the short term, there would be economic panic, rippling back through all the myriad connections, because of the sudden drop in consumption. But things would be even "worse" if such temperance during Lent were taken up as a permanent habit. There would be significant economic collapse. Too many industries depend on our overconsumption of highly processed food.

Think about it for just a painful minute. The effect

of the widespread embrace of the virtue of temperance would not just be the collapse of the fast food and junk food industry, but also everything connected with it. But even more ironic, if that many people became healthy again, losing weight through the most obvious means of eating only a moderate amount of healthy meat, fruits, and vegetables, soon enough the medical and pharmaceutical industries which have expanded to take care of our unhealthy habits would both be hit hard. The diet industry would collapse—a forty-billion-dollar-a-year industry in the US.[11] The companies that make scooter chairs for the hyper-obese would totter. In fact, there is an entire sub-industry in the medical field devoted to what's been called Bariatric Care—dealing with morbidly obese patients—and that means another related enterprise devoted to the special equipment hospitals need to deal with them, one that would crumble if temperance were embraced.[12]

And the environmental consequences? Think of all the packaging that wouldn't be thrown away if all you bought at the grocery store was healthy food. No soda bottles. No fast-food plastic forks or cardboard sandwich containers. No disposable cups and lids. No chip bags. No pre-processed, microwavable plastic, food trays. Less of those annoying plastic grocery bags, since we'd be getting fewer groceries. Intemperance and the immoderate desire for convenience not only destroy our health, they produce a lot of trash for the landfill. If we all suddenly embraced

---

[11] http://www.businessweek.com/debateroom/archives/2008/03/the_diet_industry_a_big_fat_lie.html.

[12] For a glimpse of the equipment and procedures now needed, see Shirley A. Thomas, RN, MPA, and Mary Lee-Fong, RN-C, MSN, "Maintaining Dignity of Patients with Morbid Obesity in the Hospital Setting," *Bariatric Times* 8, no. 4 (2010): 20–25.

temperance for a good solid six weeks, we wouldn't be producing nearly as much trash, and the greatly expanded garbage collecting and disposing industry would soon go into recession. The vice of intemperance is big business.

The Danger of Not Feasting

I do not wish to mislead readers into thinking that we should be continually fasting as if we were in Lent. After all, for Catholics the fasting in Lent is followed by the feasting at Easter. There are folks that become so immoderately obsessed with nutrition that they make a kind of vice out of a virtue, something like how Ebenezer Scrooge makes a vice out of thrift.

So, let me make clear that feasting is a positive, very human, and humanizing good precisely because eating, for human beings, is about more than mere nutrition: it is about romance, friendship, family, conversation, laughter, and celebration. We do not eat simply to stay alive because being alive for human beings means communion with other human beings. The Bible says that man was not meant to be alone, and so he made woman, and we can add from our common experience, that man and woman were not meant to dine alone, for eating together is part of the human romance that creates families that fill out the table.

We are social by nature, and eating together is one of the most satisfying and natural of human experiences, filling our stomachs, yes, but also our hearts with love and our minds with thoughtful conversation. Eating together is a great good; feasting together is an even greater good, because human beings, by nature, crave friendship even more than food.

That is why a recent study, which should come as no surprise, was met with such depressing dourness: because of factors like everyone flitting off here and there, the breakdown of families, the general culture of individualism, electronic devices, and no one being home to cook a meal, we eat alone over half the time.[13]

It's our natural craving for community that makes eating alone so painful and depressing. That's why the fast food companies, in their commercials, always portray people eating junk food with other people—with happy families, with laughing friends—and portray the food itself as a hyper-inviting feast as well. They are appealing—for your dining dollars—to two deeply human hungers. The sad truth is, more often than not, fast food is eaten alone, on the fly, or thrown hastily onto the kitchen table to be wolfed down by members of the household glued to their individual electronic devices.

So, I am not making a case for only eating the bare minimum of food. There's a place for feasting as well, a kind of family-centered, communal celebration that goes beyond mere nutrition, and partakes of a very healthy excess of truly wonderful food—roast turkey, roast beef cooked in red wine, mashed potatoes with butter, homemade apple pie, a glorious birthday cake! Such feasts are very human and have been occurring for nearly all of human history.

If we feasted all the time, we would, of course, be feast-

---

[13] The NPD Group, "Consumers Are Alone Over Half of Eating Occasions As A Result of Changing Lifestyles and More Single-Person Households, Reports NPD," https://www.npd.com/wps/portal/npd/us/news/press-releases/consumers-are-alone-over-half-of-eating-occasions-as-a-result-of-changing-lifestyles-and-more-single-person-households-reports-npd/.

ing to excess, and hence making ourselves obese. While there's always been feasting, there's something else going on within the last few decades that is leading to an epidemic of obesity (even while people are, more than ever before in history, eating alone). That's the kind of intemperance in regard to food that we are trying to understand in this chapter.

Rediscovering the Need for Virtue?

So, with that in mind, we may return to the important moral question. For well over two thousand years, the moderate use of worldly goods has been considered an essential moral virtue: temperance. What happened? Why does intemperance now define our culture in so many ways, including economically?

The Left is rightly disgusted and morally outraged at the results of runaway cultural intemperance. That means, for the Left, whether they admit it or not, morality isn't merely relative, a mere social construct. We can see and measure the ill effects of denying it on the environment. Much of the damage to the environment is caused by a moral failure; indeed, by the embrace of vice, not just intemperance in regard to food (gluttony) but also avarice (greed). But this makes things a bit uncomfortable, perhaps, for those on the Left. If they want to claim that sacking the environment through overconsumption is wrong—truly, undeniably wrong—they need the *real* moral distinction between virtue and vice. Moral relativism doesn't cut it, and moral relativism has been, more or less, their default view.

And the Right? They are all about morality, but they

need to embrace an uncomfortable truth: they can't champion the reality of morality without embracing the fullness of morality, not just what fits into their usual concerns. Intemperance and greed may be good for business, but vice destroys the human soul, degrades the human body, *and* befouls the beauty and integrity of God's creation. Economic "progress," defined simply by economic prosperity, might mean moral regress. Nowhere is this more clear than in the invention of hyperpalatable food.

Food Too "Good" to Be Natural

People make a lot of money from vice. As Dr. Kessler shows, the food industry has learned how to manipulate us through creating what are called hyperpalatable foods, foods that are artificially high in fat, salt, and sugar. The industry has in fact gotten the creation of hyperpalatability down to a science, a very profitable science because the more we overeat, the more money the processed food industry makes. The creation of hyperpalatable foods is one of the great causes of our obesity epidemic.

What exactly is hyperpalatability? According to Kessler, "When scientists say a food is palatable, they are referring primarily to its capacity to stimulate the appetite and prompt us to eat more."[14] Palatability is *naturally* part of foods that are good for us: think of a sweet apple, in which the nutrition of the fruit, what really feeds our hunger, is essentially united with the sweet taste, so we enjoy eating what is truly nutritious. Pretty good design, eh?

Now imagine that, by some scientific prestidigitation

---

[14] Kessler, 12.

you could extract the sweetness from the apple and throw the apple away, or even more devious, manufacture the sweet flavor through chemistry and forget the apple altogether. You've thereby created the ability to enjoy (and sell) pleasure without nutrition.

That's unnatural, especially if, on top of that, you can jack up the pleasurable taste even more, so as to hyper-stimulate our taste buds beyond what any natural food could do. "And it's that stimulation, or the anticipation of that stimulation, rather than genuine hunger, that makes us put food into our mouths long after our caloric needs are satisfied."[15]

The break between sensual pleasure and nutrition is possible, relates Kessler, because "what we eat doesn't depend solely on signals sent by the brain to maintain stable weight." There are two aspects of our bodies related to eating. One is our homeostatic, self-regulating system wherein the feeling of hunger is related to our intake of the nutrition (energy) that our body needs to maintain itself. You feel hungry; you eat; you get full; the feeling of fullness stops the desire to eat. But that's not all there is to eating. "Another region of the brain, with different circuitry, is also involved, and often it's in charge. This is known as the reward system."[16]

We animals are designed to feel the pain of hunger when we need nutritious food, just as we are designed to feel thirsty when we need water. But what motivates us to seek food is the pleasurable *reward* it gives us: the taste, texture, and smell of the food, as well as any associated pleasures that might surround it (the laughing, smiling,

---

[15] Ibid.
[16] Ibid., 10.

beautiful, happy people in the commercials). Since the two systems, while related, are separable, it is possible for animals to seek pleasurable rewards when they aren't hungry at all.

Notice I said "animals" in the above paragraph. Lots of studies have been done on rats that not only help us to understand what happens to human beings, but if you are an astute entrepreneur, also give you the scientific information you need to manipulate people like rats.

Rats Hooked on Froot Loops

As Kessler reports, just before the historical onset of hyper-obesity about the mid-twentieth century, researcher Anthony Sclafani happened to "put a rat on a lab bench near some fallen Froot Loops, the high-calorie, high-sugar cereal. He was struck by how fast the animal picked up the cereal and started to eat it." This led Sclafani to offer to the rats what he called "supermarket foods," the new, highly processed convenience foods just starting to flood the shelves. The result: rats loved it, eating way beyond what they'd normally eat in nutritional food pellets. The obvious results: fat rats, twice as heavy.[17] So, while we tend to blame nature ("It's my metabolism!"), the real cultural-economic culprit is hyperpalatable foods that drive us to eat when we are not hungry. And that's unnatural.

There is nothing in nature like a Froot Loop, where that much sweetness is united to a base structure almost entirely devoid of nutrition. "We once thought that in the absence of hunger, food could not serve as an effec-

---

[17] Ibid., 15–16.

tive reward," remarks Kessler. Naturally speaking, that is true, and gives animals and human beings a kind of natural temperance. "That idea proved to be wrong" when hyperpalatable foods were introduced, because "animals will work for foods that are high in sugar and fat even if they are not hungry." And *we* are animals. How hard will they work? "The breaking point at which the animals will no longer work for the reward" of hyperpalatable, high-sugar and -fat food "is slightly lower than the breaking point for cocaine. Animals are willing to work almost as hard to get either one."[18]

Why the unnatural pleasure high? When we eat foods high in sugar, fat, and salt, we stimulate neurons in our brain encoded to respond, by firing, to the multiple sensory characteristics of food. Ramp up the palatability, and the neurons fire more, the result being that we want more of the "food" that caused the stimulation. Remember the Lay's potato chip marketing chant: "Betcha can't eat just one!"

That's a safe bet. As you eat hyperpalatable foods, the "message to eat becomes stronger, motivating the eater to act more vigorously in pursuit of the stimulus."[19] That urgent message, the one that makes us sneak out into the kitchen for another brownie or get in our car and drive for some Doritos or fill up our carts with junk food in the grocery store, is not driven by a desire for nutrition but for the experience of ramped-up sensual pleasure itself.

---

[18] Ibid., 31.
[19] Ibid., 36.

Junk Food Junkies

The physiology allows us to see why the phrase "junk food junkie" is more appropriate than we suspected. "The neurons in the brain that are stimulated by taste and other properties of highly palatable food are part of the opioid circuitry, which is the body's primary pleasure system. The 'opioids,' also known as endorphins, are chemicals produced in the brain that have rewarding effects similar to drugs such as morphine and heroin."[20] Another brain chemical also revved up by hyper-stimulation is dopamine, which drives us all the more fervently toward our pleasure rewards.[21] As you might suspect, "dopamine . . . leads us to eat rewarding foods, which in turn stimulates the pleasure-enhancing opioid circuitry" of the brain.[22]

This means that it really is possible, in fact very common, to become a junk addict, hooked on purposely enhanced hyperpalatable foods that cause us, like the rats in the experiments, to do nearly anything to maintain that high. And addiction is the right word, as recent studies make clear.[23] According to one study, hyperpalatable

---

[20] Ibid., 37.

[21] Ibid., chaps. 8, 12.

[22] Ibid., 53.

[23] Ashley N. Gearhardt, et al., "Can food be addictive? Public health and policy implications," *Addiction* 106 (2011): 1208–1212. From p. 1208,

> The food environment has changed dramatically with the influx of hyperpalatable foods that are engineered in ways that appear to surpass the rewarding properties of traditional foods (e.g., vegetables, fruits, nuts) by increasing fat, sugar, salt, flavors and food additives to high levels. Foods share multiple features with addictive drugs. Food cues and consumption can activate neurocircuitry (e.g., meso-cortico-limbic pathways) implicated in drug addiction. Animals given intermittent access to sugar exhibit behavioral and neurobiological indicators of withdrawal and tolerance, cross-sensitization

sweeteners proved more addictive than cocaine in rats.[24]
As the authors of the study note,

> Whatever the mechanisms involved, the discovery that intense sweetness takes precedence over cocaine, one of the most addictive and harmful substances currently known, suggests that highly sweetened beverages, such as those widely available in modern human societies, may function as supernormal stimuli. . . . We speculate that the supranormal stimulation of these receptors by highly sweetened diets generates a supranormal reward, with the potential to override both homeostatic and self-control mechanisms and thus to lead to addiction.[25]

---

to psychostimulants and increased motivation to consume alcohol. Rats consuming diets high in sugar and fat demonstrate reward dysfunction associated with drug addiction, downregulation of striatal dopamine receptors and compulsive eating, including continued consumption despite receipt of shocks. In humans, diminished striatal dopamine receptor availability and striatal dysfunction have been associated with obesity and prospective weight gain. Foods and abused drugs may induce similar behavioral sequelae, including craving, continued use despite negative consequences and diminished control over consumption. If foods are capable of triggering addictive processes, applying lessons learned from drug addiction to obesity, associated metabolic problems and diet-related diseases would suggest policy directions and prevention and treatment interventions.

See also Ashley Gearhardt, Caroline Davis, Rachel Kuschner, and Kelly D. Brownell, "The Addiction Potential of Hyperpalatable Foods," *Current Drug Abuse Reviews* 4 (2011): 140–145.

[24] Magalie Lenoir, Fuschia Serre, Lauriane Cantin, and Serge H. Ahmed, "Intense Sweetness Surpasses Cocaine Reward," *PloS ONE* 8 (August 2007): 1–10.

[25] Lenoir, Serre, Cantin, and Ahmed, 6.

Moral Crimes against Nature Are Big Business

It's not difficult to see why hyperpalatability leads to obesity. Overstimulating the opioid circuitry with low-nutrition, high-calorie foods overwhelms any natural feeling of satiety, that is, of feeling full.[26] We don't stop when we would naturally stop. But that's unnatural, *literally against our nature*, as well as against the nature of the food itself—hyperpalatable food is not found in nature.[27]

By contrast, the virtue of temperance connects the natural pleasure with the natural goal: the sweetness of the apple with the nutrition. That means in our bodies our two systems are working together as well: our homeostatic, self-regulating system wherein our feeling of hunger is related to our intake of the nutrition that our body needs to maintain itself, and our pleasure-reward system. The vice of gluttony (as aided by our advanced technology) breaks that natural union, focusing only on extracting the pleasure.

That's where another vice, greed, enters. The processed and fast food industries make their money largely from breaking that connection, so that we want to "put food into our mouths long after our caloric needs are satisfied." If you've got industries making money from vice, it's obvious that consumer concern for health is bad for business. "A shrinking market for all those calories would mean less money—a lot less."[28] Hence the Lenten thought experiment.

The problems get worse as the science of hyperpalatability advances. As they get better and better at creating

---

[26] Kessler, 39.

[27] Ibid., 44.

[28] Brownell and Warner, 263.

hyperpalatability—by manipulating the sugar, fat, and salt content, along with other aspects of the flavoring and appearance—we get fatter and fatter. These companies are themselves supersized, and hence the food industry is "organized and politically powerful." Brownell and Warner continue:

> It consists of massive agribusiness companies like Cargill, Archer Daniels Midland, Bunge, and Monsanto; food sellers as large as Kraft (so big as to own Nabisco) and Pepsi-Co (owner of Frito Lay); and restaurant companies as large as McDonald's and Yum! Brands (owner of Pizza Hut, Taco Bell, KFC, and more). These are represented by lobbyists, lawyers, and trade organizations that in turn represent a type of food (e.g., Snack Food Association, American Beverage Association), a segment of the industry (e.g., National Restaurant Association), a constituent of food (e.g., Sugar Association, Corn Refiners Association), or the entire industry (e.g., Grocery Manufacturers of America).[29]

Like the tobacco industry, they resist being called on the carpet for manipulating the taste by hyperpalatability, thereby purposely making an economic killing making a wreck of consumers' health.

And it isn't just about the taste. The food industry has also figured out that by chopping up food (say, chicken in a burrito), and adding food softeners, we "consumers" are spared the time-consuming toil of chewing. That means we *eat faster*, and so eat *more*, bolting down the food before

---

[29] Ibid.

our slower, natural homeostatic nutritional system gives us the feeling of being full.

We all know that awful feeling of being way too full that we get after eating too much fast food too fast. That's the food industry's goal. As one food consultant admitted, "All of this [kind of food] has been processed such that you can wolf it down fast . . . chopped up and made ultrapalatable. . . . Very appealing looking, very high pleasure in the food, very high caloric density. . . . When you're eating these things, you've had 500, 600, 800, 900 calories before you know it."[30] These are so-called "easy calories," basically "adult baby food," with hyperpalatability enhanced by "removing the elements in whole food . . . that are harder to chew and swallow," like the apple peel missing in applesauce that's been enhanced with sugar, or the sugared cereal that has had the bran milled away.[31]

Oh, and by the way, just so we understand the full range of harm here, it turns out that sugar damages our metabolic system and our brains, disrupting fundamental neurological processes, causing brain disorders such as Alzheimer's disease, attention deficient hyperactive disorder, depression, addiction, Parkinson's disease, as well as blood pressure problems, cardiovascular disease, and, of course, obesity.[32]

If that weren't all distressing enough, it turns out that those who have a higher intake of junk food are ingesting more toxic industrial chemicals—environmental

---

[30] Quoted in Kessler, 69.

[31] Ibid., 95.

[32] Qingying Meng, et al., "Systems Nutrigenomics Reveals Brain Gene Networks Linking Metabolic and Brain Disorders," *EBiomedicine* 7 (2016): 157–166.

pollutants that become body pollutants.[33] The industrial chemicals leach into the soil; the soil feeds the plants; the plants feed the animals; we eat the animals. Obviously it's a much shorter route if we get these toxins by breathing polluted air or drinking polluted water.

---

[33] Ami R. Zota, Cassandra A. Phillips, and Susanna D. Mitro, "Recent Fast Food Consumption and Bisphenol A and Phthalates Exposures among the U.S. Population in NHANES, 2003–2010," *Environmental Health Perspectives* (April 2016): 1–33, http://ehp.niehs.nih.gov/wp-content/uploads/advpub/2016/4/ehp.1510803.acco.pdf. To clarify from the study,

> Phthalates are a class of high-production-volume industrial chemicals that are ubiquitously used in commerce. High-molecular-weight phthalates, such as di(2-ethylhexyl) phthalate (DEHP), are used as plasticizers to impart flexibility in polyvinyl chloride (PVC) materials such as food packaging, flooring, and medical devices (US Environmental Protection Agency 2012). In recent years, other phthalates, including diisononyl phthalate (DiNP), have been replacing DEHP in these applications due, in part, to legislation limiting the use of DEHP in certain applications (European Chemicals Agency 2012). Bisphenol A (BPA) is a high-production-volume chemical used to make polycarbonate plastics and epoxy resins, found in food and beverage cans as well as thermal receipt paper. . . . Experimental animal studies demonstrate that DEHP and DiNP have endocrine-disrupting properties because of their anti-androgenic effects on the male reproductive system. Human exposure to DEHP has been associated with adverse reproductive, neurobehavioral, and respiratory outcomes in children and metabolic disease risk factors such as insulin resistance in adolescents and adults. Though epidemiologic evidence of DiNP is less complete, recent studies report associations between exposure and similar health outcomes including adverse respiratory and metabolic outcomes in children. BPA is also a suspected endocrine disrupter, and experimental and human evidence suggest that BPA is a reproductive toxicant. In addition, prenatal BPA exposure has also been associated with adverse neurobehavioral outcomes in children (3–4).

Love that Bacon

Bacon should receive a lot of the blame for this—Francis Bacon, that is. Recall that in Bacon's techno-wizardry of the imaginary Salomon's House, one of his goals was to create, through scientific manipulation, "Greater pleasures of the senses." While this may *seem* a harmless goal, we can now see that it isn't.

From the standpoint of, say, Aristotle or St. Thomas Aquinas or any proponent of the importance of the virtues, the problem with enhancing the pleasures of the senses is that, in trying to break the connection between naturally-occurring pleasures and their natural goal (e.g., the good taste inherent in nutritious food), we chase after the enhanced sensation of pleasure itself as if it were the goal.

What makes us chase it all the more fervently is that today's "Food Technologists" (wouldn't Bacon be proud!) further enhance the flavors artificially by the most advanced chemistry, thereby completely cutting off any connection to the original, natural flavors—cheese flavor without the cheese, for example, or fruit taste without any fruit whatsoever.[34]

Supersizing Profits . . . and Customers

This artificial substitution allows for maximizing profits (chemical concoctions are cheaper than real food), and this is made all the worse when united with supersizing trends. As Mike McCloud, former Coca-Cola executive, related in an interview with Kessler, three decades ago "a

---

[34] Kessler, chap. 23.

triple chocolate muffin was made with real eggs, real chocolate, and real butter. It was rich and flavorful, but it was
also small."[35] But real ingredients and modest size meant
less profits, so the food industry said, "I don't want to sell a
2-ounce muffin that's made with real butter. I want to make
a 5-ounce muffin for pennies more and make more profit
on it." And so, Kessler reports, "today's muffins are much
bigger"—like the people who are eating them, we might
add—"but most of the real ingredients are gone. Instead
of butter they're likely to contain some blend of shorten-
ing and oil. . . . Powdered egg substitutes replace whole
eggs, and an array of inexpensive, processed sweeteners
are used."[36] Companies make more money with unnatural,
unreal substitutes, such as the ubiquitous high-fructose
corn syrup, a favorite hyperpalatable ingredient tied
directly to increased obesity rates,[37] one that's use has increased significantly over the last decades as obesity rates
have rocketed upward.[38]

　　Amplifying the pleasures of taste and the size of por-
tions can't help but to make it *far more* difficult for us to
be virtuous, that is, to be able to control our eating habits.
But the more difficult it is—the more we fail to control
ourselves—the more money the restaurant, snack food,
junk food, fast food, super-processed food industries
make. Coke's McCloud admits that his company pushed

---

[35] Ibid., 128. These are actually Kessler's words recounting McCloud's.

[36] Ibid., 128–129.

[37] Miriam E. Bocarsly, Elyse S. Powell, Nicole M. Avena, and Bartley G.
Hoebel, "High-fructose corn syrup causes characteristics of obesity in
rats: Increased body weight, body fat and triglyceride levels," *Pharma-
cology, Biochemistry and Behavior* 97 (2010): 101–106.

[38] Bernadette P. Marriott, Nancy Cole, and Ellen Lee, "National Estimates
of Dietary Fructose Intake Increased from 1977 to 2004 in the United
States," *Journal of Nutrition* 139 (2009): 1228S–1235S.

fast food franchises to supersize their drinks because, with so few ingredients, the profit margin on soft drinks is about 90 percent.[39] Selling a third of a gallon of soft drink makes McD's much more money.

Sinfully Delicious

Greed feeds gluttony and gluttony feeds greed; the two deadly sins mutually reinforce each other. "The food industry is not only generating billions of dollars for itself by designing hyperpalatable combinations," remarks Kessler, "it's also creating products that have the capacity to rewire our brains, driving us to seek out more and more of those products."[40]

In this instance, one could rightly say that greed is even more pernicious, since the companies are knowingly, carefully, scientifically doing everything they can to foster overindulgence in their potential customers, and hence, helping to destroy their health for the company's own profits. It is no defense, on their part, to say "The customers have free will! They don't have to eat it!" because the entire industry is aimed at breaking down customers' resistance, *so they just have to consume the product.*

As Gail Civille, president of Sensory Spectrum, proudly admits, the food industry is "trying to find the formulation that is going to make the greatest number of people want [their product]."[41] Sensory Spectrum's economic aim,

---

[39] Kessler, 129. See also Azeen Ghorayshijun, "Too Big to Chug: How Our Sodas Got So Huge," *Mother Jones,* June 25, 2012, http://motherjones.com/media/2012/06/supersize-biggest-sodas-mcdonalds-big-gulp-chart.

[40] Kessler, 137.

[41] Quoted in Kessler, 97.

as a company, is to find that formulation for its industry clients. As it boasts on its website, "Sensory Spectrum is an innovative, multi-disciplinary team of experts in the field of sensory and consumer science. We are committed to understanding every aspect of the senses and how they relate to consumer needs, wants and experiences. As consultants, we partner with our clients to provide sensory driven guidance for product development and product improvement. We offer tactical advice for product positioning, and direction for new and strategic business opportunities."[42] That's a rather long-winded way of saying, "We can help to make your product irresistible."[43]

And just so you know that there's a sub-industry of professionals dedicated to the same task, the website notifies us that the Society of Sensory Professionals recently had its conference, The 4th SSP Technical and Professional Conference, held in Tucson, AZ, the theme of which was "Influencing to Maximize Impact."[44]

One way of maximizing impact is to purposely mislead consumers about the ingredients on the labels that they "know" are bad for them, like telling what might be called little, white sugar lies. The industry puts in several different kinds of sweeteners, sugar being only one of them. If sugar were the only sweetener in, say, the cereal you bought, federal regulations demand that it has to be listed first on the label; breaking up the "sweet" means that sugar

---

[42] *Sensory Spectrum*, http://www.sensoryspectrum.com.

[43] Kessler, chap. 21.

[44] This is actually information on the 2014 SSP Conference, which the website had not yet updated. The most recent conference information can be found at the SSP website: http://www.sensorysociety.org/Pages/default.aspx.

will be listed lower.[45] Another, perhaps even more disingenuous way of misleading consumers is labeling foods as being "organic" and "all natural," and having "whole grain," when in fact, they aren't really any better at all, an example (as researchers put it) of using "unjustified health halos for highly processed and unhealthy food products."[46]

Being temperate is hard enough for us frail creatures, but the purposeful bombardment with hyperpalatable food makes virtue next to impossible. Needless to say, destroying people's capacity for virtue so you can make a lot of money is itself a sin, greed—a sin that's doubled because it would be difficult not to understand that one is also destroying people's bodily health along with it.

Adding sin to sin, the food industry (like the tobacco industry) has devised clever strategies to shift blame away from themselves, in many cases milking the Right's fears and concerns to protect their profits. These strategies include the following (which I've heard dutifully echoed by conservative talk radio hosts): "Focus on personal responsibility as the cause of the nation's unhealthy diet," "Emphasize physical activity over diet," "Raise fears that government action usurps personal freedom," and "Vilify critics with totalitarian language, characterizing them as the food police, leaders of a nanny state, and even 'food fascists,' and accuse them of desiring to strip people of their civil liberties."[47] Apparently, patriotism is the last refuge of these scoundrels. Imagine the Founding Fathers' surprise, and disgust, at the notion that brave sol-

---

[45] Kessler, 103.

[46] Temple Northup, "Truth, Lies, and Packaging: How Food Packaging Creates a False Sense of Health," *Food Studies: An Interdisciplinary Journal* 3 (March 2014): 9–18. Quote from p. 10.

[47] Brownell and Warner, 265.

diers shed their blood so we could drink sixty-four-ounce fizzy drinks.

While we ponder the destruction of our health, let's not forget the ill effects that all this has on the environment: all the trash, all the waste, that comes from all phases of production, packaging, delivery, consumption, and, finally, the tossing into the landfill—or, if you have forgotten it, read the previous chapter again.

A Disquieting Addendum for the Left

But here's some other food for thought, a morsel that will be eminently indigestible to all too many in our society. If we map, historically, the sharp rise of obesity in the United States in the latter third of the twentieth century, along with the origin and explosive growth of the junk food, fast food, and processed food industries during the same time, and then map the sharp increase of women entering the workforce which happened during the same period, we find that they coincide. Listen to Eric Schlosser, author of *Fast Food Nation: The Dark Side of the All-American Meal*:

> In 1975, about one-third of American mothers with young children worked outside the home; today almost two-thirds of such mothers are employed. As the sociologists Cameron Lynne Macdonald and Carmen Sirianni have noted, the entry of so many women into the workforce has greatly increased demand for the types of services that housewives traditionally performed: cooking, cleaning, and child care. A generation ago, three-quarters of the

money used to buy food in the United States was spent to prepare meals at home. Today about half of the money used to buy food is spent at restaurants—mainly at fast food restaurants.[48]

And not just restaurants. Given two parents both working outside the home or single-parent homes, the default purchase of food from the grocery store has to be highly processed, hyperpalatable convenience food that takes little time to prepare, with all the packaging that goes to the landfill, and the cacophony of chemicals that goes into our bodies. Cooking real food from scratch every night, or even once a week, can't be done under such conditions.

Small wonder that we dine alone and on the go, or wolf down food while looking at our smartphones even if we happen to be one of the few American families that actually sits around the same table for something resembling dinner. The regular, careful, and loving preparation of homemade food, whether it is for a regular dinner or a feast, is one very human thing that disappeared with the push of women outside the home. It is, in fact, one of the reasons why our houses are no longer homes.

A Disquieting Addendum for the Right

Since I've introduced an additional heavy dose of moral ambiguity here, we might as well pile on another, which helps us to see why the largest sense of ecology—the

---

[48] Eric Schlosser, *Fast Food Nation: The Dark Side of the All-American Meal* (Boston: Mariner Books, 2012), 4.

Catholic sense—must look at the entire web of causes and effects of our choices and actions.

As Schlosser also makes painfully clear, the result of the sharp rise in convenience food—and what is more convenient than stopping by MacDonald's after work, *again*, to grab supper for the family—caused an equally notable spike in industries that supply its ingredients. Looks like good economics, doesn't it? A "rising tide lifts all ships" kind of thing, as the Right is so fond of saying?

Let's look at beef production, since the hamburger is our favorite fast food. What has actually occurred over the last few decades is a push on suppliers by fast food corporations to provide enormous quantities of meat, and to do so *as cheaply as possible*. And the way to do that is to construct vast factories that employ unskilled labor in dangerous and squalid conditions, all for low pay. You don't get a cheap burger otherwise.

So, visit one of these "burger factories," and you witness the following: There's the "knocker," the "man who welcomes cattle to the building. Cattle walk down a narrow chute and pause in front of him, blocked by a gate, and then he shoots them in the head with a captive bolt stunner. . . . For eight and a half hours, he just shoots." And another happy employee: "For eight and a half hours, a worker called a 'sticker' does nothing but stand in a river of blood, being drenched in blood, slitting the neck of a steer every ten seconds or so, severing its carotid artery." The folks that cut up the meat are covered in chain mail because it is such a dangerous job, and they are compelled to do it at dizzying speed, about a cut every three seconds—hence the high injury rate. Every year one in three workers in meatpacking requires medical attention beyond first aid, including not only lacerations of all kinds, but back and neck injuries, carpal tunnel syndrome, fingers unable to bend from a trigger-finger position. Even the clean-up crews are subject to dangers: sniffing toxic fumes, working in temperatures up to 100 degrees, being sprayed with burning cleaning chemicals. Few Americans would work under such conditions, which is why the meat-processing industry loves immigrants. They're low-pay and disposable.[49]

The mega-poultry industry isn't much better. I recall, when we lived in Minnesota, the horrible conditions endured by undocumented Mexican immigrants lured up to the local turkey processing plants with promises of American riches. They stand in cold rooms up to their ankles in water, blood, and guts, disemboweling and slicing up turkeys all day.

It's no better in the chicken processing industry, as a recent report by Oxfam makes clear. "While the poultry industry today enjoys record profits and pumps out billions of chickens, the reality of life inside the processing plant remains grim and dangerous. Workers earn low wages, suffer elevated rates of injury and illness, toil in difficult conditions, and have little voice in the workplace."[50] One of the most unpleasant things suffered is that the push to produce is so unrelenting, that workers are not allowed to stop and go to the bathroom. "Workers struggle to cope with this denial of a basic human need. They urinate and defecate while standing on the line; they wear diapers to work; they restrict intake of liquids and fluids to danger-

---

[49] Ibid., chap. 8.

[50] Oxfam, "No Relief: Denial of Bathroom Breaks in the Poultry Industry," https://www.oxfamamerica.org/static/media/files/No_Relief_Embargo.pdf.

ous degrees; they endure pain and discomfort while they worry about their health and job security. And it's not just their dignity that suffers: they are in danger of serious health problems."[51]

Think about that when downing those Chicken Mc-Nuggets next time.

What Have We Learned about Ecology?

So what does this all mean for our assessment of the broadest and deepest understanding of ecology, one defined by the whole interconnected web that includes the natural world, the human body and soul, and our moral and economic nature?

First of all, we are animals, animals who take in food for nutrition. Like other animals, we are also blessed with a self-regulating homeostatic system that governs our bodies' intake of food and its metabolism. We also have a reward system that pushes us, through pleasure, to procure the food we need. Both systems are meant to work in union for our health, and as long as nothing unnatural happens, they do.

While we are indeed animals, we are a very special, quite distinct kind of animal—a rational animal whose actions can emanate from free will rather than from instinct, and who has the capacity to alter nature by his reason. But these gifts make it possible for us—alone among all the animals—to technologically separate the nutritional goal of eating from the pleasure, and become all-absorbed in the pleasure. Rats can't do it for them-

---

[51] Ibid.

selves any more than any other kind of animal. But they show us the results of our folly in the lab, and make it clear that this unnatural separation is addictive self-destruction. Poor rats. Foolish humans.

But secondly, we have seen an intrinsic, intricate moral strand in this web, or better, several strands. Animals can't, by themselves, engage in massive, self-destructive eating behaviors because they can only eat what they get in the wild, where pleasurable flavors that entice them are natural to the food they should eat. They aren't subject to the natural possibility of the vice of gluttony. Nor do we blame the poor, fat rats frantically waddling, wide-eyed and slavering, towards the trove of Froot Loops at the end of a maze. They are gluttons by human manipulation, and so carry no moral blame. But we do censure our own capacity to overeat as a vice—gluttony—and even more, we morally blame those who knowingly manipulate us like lab rats, preying on and exacerbating our weaknesses, for their own fat economic profits. We also blame those— and here the Left is dead on right—who, in the name of "economic progress," glibly ignore all the evidence of the destruction of our health by an economy largely fueled by super-corporations pushing hyperpalatable overconsumption, as well as the degradation of the environment brought about by the ever-increasing mountains of garbage such overconsumption produces as waste.

These moral censures make no sense, however, if we are not somehow something beyond a mere animal, for no animal can be morally blamed for its actions. That moral dimension is not possible if, in accordance with modern secular thought, we are just one more kind of animal, a life-support system for just one more random variation of DNA.

It would seem, then, that the Left would want to take another look at its default atheism if it wants to hold to the moral high road, and the Right had better take a more honest look at the immoral effects of so-called economic progress.

And if you think that's all painful enough, wait 'til we look at sex, another very interesting aspect of our animal nature that's been thoroughly trashed.

CHAPTER FIVE

The Pollution of Sex

Wall·E, *Dehumanization, and the Death of Romance*

And now the sex thing. Is there such a thing as the destruction of the sexual landscape? If we can befoul nature by violating its intrinsic order and beauty, can we do the same to human nature and in particular human sexuality? If intemperance and greed destroy the natural environment, do they also destroy the moral environment and sexuality itself?

This is a difficult question for the Left because it has generally viewed the liberation of sexual desire *from* traditional moral constraints as unquestionably good, and chemistry and technology as the instruments for achieving this complete sexual freedom.

But in what way is that any different from liberating the desire for ever more exotic and chemically enhanced junk food from human health? Why is the technologically-enabled absorption into hyperpalatable food—brought about by separating the sensual pleasure from the nutrition, and hyper-stimulating the pleasure-based reward system at the expense of health—any different from the technologically-enabled absorption into sexual pleasure? Why is it that the Left can speak of the harm of acting the natural order in regard to the environment, t the possible harm of acting against the natural order in the moral environment?

I mentioned that in *Wall·E* human obesity is a sign of dehumanization. One sign of this dehumanization is degenderization. On the spaceship *Axiom* the natural distinction between male and female—quite evident in other animal pairs—has been all but erased. Everyone is soft, round, and has breasts. Sex-based differences have nearly disappeared. This is not fiction, nor is it limited to losing a naturally distinctive male or female shape. One effect of obesity in males is loss of fertility due to a significant drop in testosterone production.[1] Another effect in men is increased production of the female hormone estrogen.[2]

In *Wall·E*, another result of this junk-food induced androgyny is that there is no human romance, a defect intensified by computer addiction. Males and females have lost all desire for each other because they spend all their days jetting around on the scooter chairs, eating and gossiping while they stare at the electronic screens in front of them. Screens have replaced real human contact, including romantic contact.

---

[1] See, e.g., Mara Y. Roth, John K. Amory, and Stephanie T. Page, "Treatment of male infertility secondary to morbid obesity," *Nature Clinical Practice Endocrinology & Metabolism* 4 (2008): 415–419; Mark Ng Tang Fui, Philippe Dupuis, and Mathis Grossmann, "Lowered testosterone in male obesity: mechanisms, morbidity and management," *Asian Journal of Andrology* 16, no. 2 (March–April 2014): 223–231; and Stefan S. Du Plessis, et al., "The effect of obesity on sperm disorders and male infertility," *Nature Reviews Urology* 7 (March 2010): 153–161. See also Charles Faiman, "Male Hypogonadism" (June 2012), http://www.clevelandclinicmeded.com/medicalpubs/diseasemanagement/endocrinology/male-hypogonadism/.

[2] G. Schneider, M. A. Kirschner, R. Berkowitz, and N. H. Ertel, "Increased estrogen production in obese men," *Journal of Clinical Endocrinology and Metabolism* 48, no. 4 (April 1979): 633–638.

Not only is romance gone, but also its natural aim, sexual reproduction. The children on the *Axiom* are not even the result of sexuality. Although it is never explicitly explained, babies seem to be one more thing produced artificially through *Buy 'n' Large* technology. Since males and females, in this artificial world, have no biological goal—after all, any biologist can tell us that in all other animals the deep biological distinction between male and female, and the sexual desires that follows upon it, have their meaning and natural end in the reproduction of young—the distinct human sexes fade into androgyny. Just as their feet have become vestigial organs, so also their primary and secondary biological-sexual organs seem to have become vestigial as well.

Hyperpalatable Porn

Of course, *Wall·E* is a kids' movie, so even though it edges into deeper waters, it can't take its social satire in regard to sexuality into the darker destruction of human sexuality that has taken place in our culture. We all know what would *really* happen on a spaceship with everyone addicted to screens: what has already happened here and now, the destruction of natural sexuality through unnatural pornography. As with the food industry, the porn industry knows that creating addiction through hyperpalatability—supranormal sexual stimulation untethered from any goal other than maximizing individual sensual pleasure—is immensely profitable.

In order to understand the porn revolution we've got to understand that it's the culmination of the sexual revolution that, along with the transformation of food, is part of the Baconian-inspired philosophical revolution. This revolution sought to redefine human nature and nature itself by a materialist worldview, one which reduces human beings entirely to pleasure- and comfort-seeking, pain- and discomfort-avoiding beings. The pathological focus on the pleasures of food and the pleasures of sex, technologically extracted from their natural foundations, is the end result of the Baconian attempt to master nature.

This revolution doesn't fulfill, but rather degrades human beings. A sign of the unnaturalness of this degradation is that in both morbid obesity and porn addiction human beings fall below the level of animals. Apart from when they are connected to human beings—like fat, little lapdogs continually fed by plumper elderly women, or rats in lab experiments with Froot Loops—no other animal becomes morbidly obese. And while animals have seasons of heat that are not PG viewing (because of the wildness of the sex and sometimes for the brutality of the violence that accompanies it) their sex is aimed toward and limited by their natural goal of reproduction.

But human beings (mainly males) have recently become so obsessed by and addicted to porn use that they prefer, by far, a combination of the screen and masturbation to an actual, flesh and blood human female. The effect can be characterized as what University of Pennsylvania psychologist Dr. Mary Anne Layden calls "sexual obesity," the self-destructive gorging on sexual pleasure.[3]

---

[3]   See Mary Anne Layden's paper, "Sexual Obesity: Research on the Public Health Crisis of Pornography," available at http://endsexualexploitation. org/wp-content/uploads/NCSE-Capitol-Briefing_Mary-Anne-Layden_ Sexual-Obesity-Research-on-the-Public-Health-Crisis-of-Pornogra-phy_07-14-2015.pdf. I first ran across Layden's work, and the concept of "sexual obesity," in Mary Eberstadt's *Adam and Eve after the Pill: Paradoxes of the Sexual Revolution* (San Francisco: Ignatius, 2012), 56.

And porn addiction isn't just self-destructive. As we'll see, it kills marriages and destroys families; it fuels prostitution and hence human trafficking; it uses and abuses real woman, real men, real girls, real boys and then throws them away; it spirals downward into ever more bizarre and violent, sexually unnatural acts to satisfy the deadened libidos of ever more warped consumers for whom pleasure-seeking has gone so wild that it seeks pain and even the death of its victim; and if that weren't enough, it ends in males with complete erectile dysfunction. Such are the smoldering ashes of the sexual revolution.

There were two key pieces of technology that allowed for the sexual revolution to take place: the first was effective contraception (primarily the Pill), and the second was the invention of the computer that gave us the Internet. The former uncoupled sexual pleasure from its biological foundation in procreation in the same way that, in regard to the junk and fast food industry, the sweetness was extracted from the naturally nutritious food. The latter delivers porn to anyone with a smartphone. The pleasure itself thereby became the increasingly obsessive, and hence addictive, focus.

This is unnatural, that is, against nature. Pleasure is natural to sexual intercourse that produces young—a fact we may have forgotten—just as a real apple off the tree or tomato out of the garden gives both pleasure and natural nutrition. But in trying to steal the pleasure itself, the desire-seeking part of us has been cut loose, and we have become, quite literally, ever more sexually aimless and unnatural. Let's examine these assertions by looking first at the *nature* of sexuality.

Sex by the (Biology) Book

How about beginning with a basic biology textbook, since we should assume that nature, our nature, gives us some clue about what we are and how we should act? We are mammals, so the book tells us. "All mammals reproduce by internal fertilization: The male releases sperm into the female's reproductive tract where one or more eggs are fertilized."[4] I suspected as much.

And if we might trust the diagrams in the text, there seems to be some different equipment for this, divided roughly along the lines of gender.[5] I won't include the details in this book because they are readily available to anyone who cares to look—and we *should* care to look. Biologists are not blinded, generally, by a program of sexual liberation. They describe exactly what sex is for, and do so in terms of the natural distinction between male and female that we find throughout nature. If we are going to approach ecology from this obvious beginning point of elementary biology, we should approach our moral ecology in regard to sexuality from here as well. To do otherwise would not be scientific.

It is scientific to understand that gender, male and female, is a real natural category. Any competent biology textbook will point out the obvious. When we look at our respective biological parts, the sexes are complementary

---

[4] George Johnson and Peter Raven, *Biology* (Orlando, FL: Hold, Rinehart and Winston, 2004), 808.

[5] "What are the roles of a male in mammalian sexual reproduction? Recall that sexual reproduction involves the formation of a diploid zygote from two haploid cells, or gametes, through fertilization. The roles of a male in sexual reproduction are to produce sperm cells—the male gametes—and to deliver the sperm cells to the female reproductive system to fertilize an egg cell—the female gamete" (Johnson and Raven, 996).

by nature. If, for example, we examine the female side of sexual reproductive biology, we find out that a female has exactly *not* the parts that we find on a male, but biological parts that *complement* those in a male, and these female parts are defined by the internal fertilization and growth of an egg. The two, by nature, complete each other, as they do in all animals that reproduce in this way.

This much all should be obvious *biologically*. Whatever we might be doing sexually (just as whatever we might happen to be eating), sexuality is by nature defined by an intricate system designed for procreation, creating other members of the same species (just as eating is naturally aimed at nutrition). The natural pleasure entailed serves the goal. It makes animals want to mate. It is the obvious natural foundation of human marriage.

But Where's the Romance?

Husbands and wives will, of course, object to ending things there. Marriage is more than merely a means for reproduction. It is a union of two bodies and two souls, a man and a woman who each find completion in a union of lifelong love, so that even the sexual act bears with it not just sensual pleasure but joy, a joy that celebrates their own deepening love for each other and the fruit of that union in their children. Just as food is for the sake of nutrition, but also, given our distinctly human capacities, for the sake of feasting, so also the sexual union in marriage is a kind of feast, a celebration of the deepest possible human friendship, the friendship of a husband and wife which creates more guests at the table.

All true, very, very true. In previously making clear

natural, biological foundation of sexuality, I do not in any way wish to reduce human sexuality merely to the foundation. That is the error of materialist reductionism. The truth is precisely the reverse: our sexual biology leads us upward, even in regard to biological aspects we share with other animals.

To take the male side of things again, the "pleasure" neurotransmitter dopamine is released from the tegmentum section in our midbrain in response to romantic cues by the wife—her pretty face, a certain mischievous smile—which are picked up by the sight and processed by the brain's lateral geniculate nucleus, resulting in romantic arousal, beginning with the release of dopamine. The dopamine in smaller doses enhances the feeling of anticipatory pleasure and focuses the man intensely on his wife beforehand, and is also released in greater amounts at consummation, causing a flood of pleasure.

But that's not all that biology does to prepare the feast of romance. The release of the male hormone testosterone and the neurotransmitter norepinephrine both increase the anticipation and further focuses the man on his wife. Norepinephrine enhances the experience because it is also involved in storing important "emotional stimuli." As biopsychologist William Struthers notes, "Norepinephrine burns the object that initiated the arousal into our memories because of its physiological and emotional significance," thereby producing deep and happy emotional memories that fuel further romance between the spouses. "We were designed to store significant experiences of sexual intimacy with norepinephrine's help,"[6]

---

[6] William Struthers, *Wired for Intimacy: How Pornography Hijacks the Male Brain* (Downers Grove, IL: InterVarsity Press, 2009), 103.

each marital feast provisioning for those in the future.

But there's more to the husband's experience of romance. The flood of dopamine at consummation also, interestingly enough, simultaneously shuts down the amygdala, the part of our brain dealing with fear, anxiety, and anger. The experience of euphoric pleasure via dopamine and the complete shut-down of fear, anxiety, and anger are made for each other, we might say, or better, made for the couple. Just to make sure the intimate euphoria is overflowing, endogenous opiates are also released, which suppress any pain one might be having from other sources. The joy and love of the marital union are biologically reinforced all the more because oxytocin and vasopressin are released throughout the romantic encounter, and in a rush at its euphoric consummation, the former enhancing the great feeling of satisfaction and the latter actually binding the husband to his wife.[7] That's not a bad design, to say the least!

Sexual Destruction and Moral Pollution

We love with our whole being, body and soul, in the union of man and woman as husband and wife. And that is what

---

[7] See the excellent account in Struthers, chap. 4. See also Larry Young, "The Neural Basis of Pair Bonding in a Monogamous Species: A Model for Understanding the Biological Basis of Human Behavior" in *Offspring: Human Fertility Behavior in Biodemographic Perspective*, National Research Council, Division of Behavioral and Social Sciences and Education, Committee on Population, Panel for the Workshop on the Biodemography of Fertility and Family Behavior, Kenneth W. Wachter, and Rodolfo A. Bulatao, eds., (Washington, DC: National Academies Press, 2003), https://www.ncbi.nlm.nih.gov/books/NBK97287/#_ch4_s4; and Thomas Insel, "The Challenge of Translation in Social Neuroscience: A Review of Oxytocin, Vasopressin, and Affiliative Behavior," *Neuron* 65 (March 25, 2010): 768–779.

makes it a feast. We're made for romance that finds its culmination in this most fundamental of human unions. But porn deeply wounds and sometimes kills the whole thing. It is the most toxic pollution of our sexual nature, and I focus on the male side of things because males are addicted to porn in greater proportion, and therefore there is much more research showing its harmful effects. (But as more and more women become addicted, we'll be finding complementary studies increasing as well.)

I have warned the Right that it is a moral failure to ignore evidence that our activities, even those that enhance us economically, are actually self-destructive and immoral. Feverish overconsumption creates massive mountains of ugly, toxic garbage—it doesn't matter whether the landfills are in someone else's backyard. Junk food and fast food certainly make America economically strong, but they're also destructive. "Out of sight, out of mind" is an infantile approach, and conveniently forgets the real damage done to our bodies (which, I assume, you on the Right may still hold to be temples) and to the natural world (which, I assume, some of you still hold to be God's creation).

The Left rightly rejects these all-too-typical ways of not taking moral responsibility for our actions in regard to nature. But what about the evidence that the sexual revolution has, in fact, not liberated us, but is creating just as much ugliness and destruction as other forms of pollution in regard to human nature? You on the Left must take your moral medicine as well.

As the first dose, I'm going to focus on the destruction caused by pornography because the masturbatory narcissistic solipsism in which it has ended is the exact opposite of the natural biological goal of the misused organs involved.

Maybe It Actually Does Cause Blindness— or Worse

Ahem. Here goes. There is, quite literally, a worldwide epidemic of erectile dysfunction (ED) among young men, men less than forty years old. While it is quite natural to have problems of this sort in men over forty (although it has been made worse by increasing obesity and the diabetes that often comes with it), a significant rise in the number of young men with ED is historically unprecedented. In one study, one in four men seeking treatment for ED was under forty years old—setting off an alarm for clinicians.[8] In another, a third of young men were suffering from sexual dysfunction.[9] A study (in Italy) uncovered a doubling of ED in teenagers in just eight years (2005–2013).[10] A study in Canada found that over 50 percent of male teens reported some ED symptoms, with half of those being severe.[11] There are several causal factors, including increased obesity in the young, as well as the use of illegal drugs, but one cause stands out with great clarity: the worldwide epidemic of ED is made possible by the worldwide availability of Internet porn coupled with obsessive masturbation.[12]

---

[8] Paolo Capogrosso, et al., "One Patient out of Four with Newly Diagnosed Erectile Dysfunction Is a Young Man—Worrisome Picture from the Everyday Clinical Practice," *Journal of Sexual Medicine* 10 (2013): 1833–1841.

[9] Anaïs Mialon, et al., "Sexual Dysfunctions Among Young Men: Prevalence and Associated Factors," *Journal of Adolescent Health* 51 (2012): 25–31.

[10] Quoted in Gary Wilson, *Your Brain on Porn: Internet Pornography and the Emerging Science of Addiction* (Kent, UK: Commonwealth, 2014), 29–30.

[11] Lucia F. O'Sullivan, et al., "Prevalence and Characteristics of Sexual Functioning among Sexually Experienced Middle to Late Adolescents," *Journal of Sexual Medicine* 11 (2014): 630–641.

[12] See the excellent Gary Wilson, *Your Brain on Porn*, chap. 1, which has an extensive bibliography, as well as copious material from Internet

Internet porn has the same effect as hyperpalatable junk food: it increases the pleasure to unnatural levels, severing it from any other goal than maximizing pleasure, thereby causing addiction. Sexual addiction, as such, is not new, and neither is pornography—there was pornography in ancient Rome, and a resurgence of pornography with the modern invention of the printing press.[13] The difference today is that with the invention of the Internet, the availability, the intensity, and the unnaturalness of pornography have exploded exponentially, creating, in the words of researchers Jennifer Riemersma and Michael Sytsma, "a toxic cocktail of contemporary addiction."[14]

Typically, *in the past*, sexual addicts had troubled childhoods, almost all (97 percent) of the addicts themselves being victims of emotional abuse, over 70 percent being physically abused, and over 80 percent sexually abused.[15] They came from dysfunctional, loveless families, and latched onto sex as a kind of drug, resulting in "compulsive sexual behavior that results in tolerance, escalation, withdrawal, and a loss of volitional control despite neg-

---

sites devoted to men who are trying to break the porn habit, in great part, because of severe ED. See also Tyger Latham, Psy.D., "Does Porn Contribute to ED?" *Psychology Today* (May 3, 2012), https://www.psychologytoday.com/blog/therapy-matters/201205/does-porn-contribute-ed; and Hannah James and Sean O'Shea, "Porn Causing Erectile Dysfunction in Young Men," *Global News* (March 30, 2014), http://globalnews.ca/news/1232726/porn-causing-erectile-dysfunction-in-young-men/.

[13] See my *Worshipping the State: How Liberalism Became Our State Religion* (Washington, DC: Regnery, 2013), chap. 2.

[14] Jennifer Riemersma and Michael Sytsma, "A New Generation of Sexual Addiction," *Sexual Addiction & Compulsivity* 20 (2013): 306–322, p. 307. For a short history of the concept of sexual addiction see pp. 307–308.

[15] Ibid., 309.

ative consequences."[16] Toxic families created the perfect dysfunctional matrix for future sex addicts. Interestingly, food addiction can lead to, or amplify, sexual addiction: gluttony fuels lust, one vice feeds another.[17]

But contemporary sex addicts break this predictive correlation: with the advent of the Internet, and the acidic ubiquity of porn, more and more addicts are created from those who have had quite normal childhoods. "Contemporary sexual addiction is unique in that, where access to technology is present, all ages, cultures, genders, races, socioeconomic levels, and education levels appear equally affected." The flood of porn washes over everyone, creating addiction in younger and younger children—the first exposure to porn now being about ten years old.[18] Just so you know how evil porn peddlers are, they set up links to "pornography websites with names that mirror common misspellings of children's Web searches."[19] They hook them early, just like the junk food industry.

Recall how hyperpalatable food hijacks and unnaturally intensifies the reward-seeking part of the brain. Porn does the same. "The brain registers all pleasures in the same way," a Harvard Mental Health Newsletter explains,

> whether they originate with a psychoactive drug, a monetary reward, a sexual encounter, or a satisfying meal. In the brain, pleasure has a distinct

---

[16] Ibid., 308.

[17] Ibid., 310. On the physiological connection between lust and gluttony, and drug use as well, see Elaine Hull, "Sex, drugs and gluttony: How the brain controls motivated behaviors," *Physiology & Behavior* 104 (2011): 173–177.

[18] Ibid., 311.

[19] Ibid.

signature: the release of the neurotransmitter dopamine in the nucleus accumbens, a cluster of nerve cells lying underneath the cerebral cortex. Dopamine release in the nucleus accumbens is so consistently tied with pleasure that neuroscientists refer to the region as the brain's pleasure center. . . . dopamine interacts with another neurotransmitter, glutamate, to take over the brain's system of reward-related learning. This system has an important role in sustaining life because it links activities needed for human survival (such as eating and sex) with pleasure and reward. The reward circuit in the brain includes areas involved with motivation and memory as well as with pleasure. Addictive substances *and* behaviors stimulate the same circuit—and then overload it.[20]

Repeated exposure—the click, click, click of the computer mouse, coupled with masturbation—both makes us seek the pleasure ever more passionately and, simultaneously, dulls the feeling of pleasure we get, so that ever more bizarre and unnatural stimuli are needed for the fix. Either having or viewing natural sex—actual male-female intercourse—no longer satisfies. The spiral ends in ED and even with the complete deadening of the libido—the destruction of the very organ of sexual desire by solipsistic sex.

---

[20] Harvard Health Publications, "How addiction hijacks the brain" (July, 2011), http://www.health.harvard.edu/newsletter_article/how-addiction-hijacks-the-brain. Emphasis added.

Becoming Ever More Morally Blind: Defining Sexual Tolerance Down

So much for the notion that masturbation and porn are equally harmless. The toxic union of the two allows us to become both physiologically degraded and morally blind, the dual effect of what is technically termed "tolerance." As scientists now understand, addiction of any kind, including sexual addiction, "hijacks" the brain's natural reward system.

In a person who becomes addicted, brain receptors become overwhelmed. The brain responds by producing less dopamine or eliminating dopamine receptors—an adaptation similar to turning the volume down on a loudspeaker when noise becomes too loud.

As a result of these adaptations, dopamine has less impact on the brain's reward center. People who develop an addiction typically find that, in time, the desired substance no longer gives them as much pleasure. They have to take more of it to obtain the same dopamine high because their brains have adapted—an effect known as *tolerance*.[21]

Tolerance is part of addiction, and as researcher Nora Volkow and her colleagues state succinctly, "addiction is a disease of the brain . . . characterized by an expanding cycle of dysfunction."[22]

(handwritten margin note: on not!)

---

[21] Harvard Health Publications. Emphasis added. See also Nora Volkow, "Addiction: Decreased reward sensitivity and increased expectation sensitivity conspire to overwhelm the brain's control circuit," *Bioessays* 32 (2010): 748–755; and Eric Nestler, "Is there a common molecular pathway for addiction?" *Nature Neuroscience* 8, no. 11 (November 2005): 1445–1449.

[22] Volkow, 748–749. For a very helpful overview of the research that has been done, conclusively marking porn addiction as a real addiction, see Todd Love, et al., "Neuroscience of Internet Pornography Addiction: A

But with the dysfunction of porn addiction, tolerance has two related meanings. First, it refers to the need for greater and greater, harder and harder porn to achieve the high, and second, tolerance causes a destructive effect on the viewer of porn morally—*he or she becomes socially tolerant of ever more unnatural and destructive sexual behaviors.*

As a result of increased tolerance in both senses, every sexual combination or variation is now available on the Internet, both creating and responding to the demands of the addicted: sex with any gender combination, including transgender; vaginal, oral, anal, and masturbatory sex; sex with objects; sex with animals; sex involving participants wearing diapers; sex involving feces or urine; amputee sex; sex involving choking and vomiting, brutal sadism, torture, rape, and even murder; cartoon pornography and child pornography; and finally, computer generated virtual sex of any and every unnatural and previously unimaginable kind.[23]

We can map the degrading effect of tolerance on pornographic films over the last several decades. As Natalie Purcell has shown in depressing, nauseating detail, porn movies over the last forty years have become increasingly violent and misogynist, with women being choked, suffocated, dragged by the hair, gang raped, slapped, punched, gagged through oral sex to the point of vomiting, and humiliated in other ways that I have not the courage or the stomach to report (much of it dealing with hideously disgusting variations of anal intercourse). The women either pretend to love it (the more abusive the better), or the women are shown actually suffering in their painful humil-

Review and Update," *Behavioral Sciences* 5 (2015): 388–433.
[23] Riemersma and Sytsma, 312–313.

iation as real rape victims, both of which are meant to "turn on" porn addicts seeking new highs, both of which form the brains of porn viewers to associate their own sexual satisfaction with brutal and unnatural violations of women.[24]

Sexual variety is not the spice of life. The variety of porn offerings on the Internet fuels the addiction, the addict goes in search of ever more unnatural variety as he or she becomes more "tolerant,"[25] accepting of the sexually unnatural as normal.

Here, "accepting" is too vague a term. As I just noted, what happens is the fusion of the porn-viewer's sexual desire with the unnatural, supranormal, violent, disgusting stimuli, thereby literally remaking his brain and his sexual appetite in terms of what he views, so that he now

---

[24] Natalie Purcell, *Violence and the Pornographic Imaginary: The Politics of Sex, Gender, and Aggression in Hardcore Pornography* (New York: Routledge, 2012).

[25] See Matthias Brand, Jan Snagowski, Christian Laier, and Stefan Maderwald, "Ventral striatum activity when watching preferred pornographic pictures is correlated with symptoms of Internet pornography addiction," *NeuroImage* 129 (2016): 224–232, especially p. 230:

> The Internet provides endless opportunities to find pornographic material that fits with individual fantasies. Thus, individuals with specific sexual preferences or fantasies could develop a loss of control over their pornography use, because brain systems involved in reward anticipation respond in particular to those pictures or videos that are more preferred than others. This can potentially result in a vicious circle, whereby neural reward anticipation systems provide motivational drive to find material that fits increasingly better with individuals' preferences. This mechanism would remain active, as individuals can never be sure that there is no material on the Internet that is even closer to their personal desire than that currently seen. Several media-specific characteristics are potential contributing factors including convenience and anonymity of pornography use, affordability, accessibility, and the chance to escape from reality. . . .

feels sexual desire is satiable only in terms of where he is on the sliding scale of degeneration into the hardest porn. *That means that we, culturally, are reforming the sexual desire of men to want to rape women.*

Not too surprisingly, porn addicts who do in fact hold to the Judeo-Christian sexual moral code are intolerant of their own behavior. Unlike the unreligious, they *understand* that they are addicted, because they believe that viewing pornography is *wrong*.[26] But tolerance in both senses is increasingly eroding this social-moral code because the results of porn viewing do not stay private. Private acts have social and political effects, *like toxins leaking from a landfill.* Thus, the moral culture has changed just as drastically and quickly during the very period that the Internet saturated and transformed everything about us. As Riemersma and Sytsma note,

> Cultural sexual mores in the United States have changed rapidly in the last generation. Highly sexualized images and themes are commonly used in advertising, television, movies, and music, such that it is impossible to avoid repeated exposure on a daily basis. Everything from computers to phones to video-game consoles provides one-touch access to the Internet and therefore to graphic pornog-

---

[26] Joshua Grubbs, "Transgression as Addiction: Religiosity and Moral Disapproval as Predictors of Perceived Addiction to Pornography," *Archives of Sexual Behavior* 44 (2015): 125–136. According to the study, "Religiosity predicted more negative moral attitudes about pornography use, which in turn predicted greater perceived addiction," so that, to state what should be obvious, the "association between religiosity and perceived addiction is likely accomplished through the relationship that religiosity has with sexual values and moral disapproval of certain sexual behaviors" (133–134).

raphy, sexually explicit websites, chat rooms, and even sexual gaming and virtual sexual worlds.[27]

Technology and money drives this moral transformation. The economic and technological development of the Internet and porn are intricately connected: indeed, pornography is the "single most influential economic engine" driving the technological and economic development.[28] Porn gave us advanced e-commerce capabilities, high-quality video streaming, webcams, increased bandwidth, among other things.[29] It brings in billions and billions of dollars. Ten years ago, $57 billion globally.[30] Who knows how much now? One reasonable estimate is $97 billion.[31] But one thing is very clear. Two of the seven deadly sins unite in this dance of destruction: greed drives lust, vice fuels vice, creating an ever-larger and more damaging flame.

Demonstrating the Deeper Destruction of Porn Pollution

Here, we must be much more exact and thorough about the real destruction porn causes. Just as the Right often wants to believe that there are no bad effects of industrial and economic expansion, so also the Left wants to believe

[27] Riemersma and Sytsma, 313.

[28] Anthony Jack, "Foreword" in Wilson, xi.

[29] Patchen Barss, "Ten indispensable technologies built by the pornography industry," *Enterprise Features*, http://www.enterprisefeatures.com/ ten-indispensable-technologies-built-by-the-pornography-industry/.

[30] Riemersma and Sytsma, 313.

[31] Chris Morris, "Things Are Looking Up in America's Porn Industry," *NBC News*, January 20, 2015, http://www.nbcnews.com/business/ business-news/things-are-looking-americas-porn-industry-n289431/.

that there are no bad effects of the release of sexuality from moral constraints. And both loudly proclaim, "I have a right to. . . ."

In both cases, in order to assess them morally we must ask: are there bad effects of these actions? How do we know? Privately-produced trash does in fact cause pollution, which demonstrably harms nature. And the reason that we know that junk food is bad for us is that it causes actual, significant destruction to our health. Our health is defined by what our body is, its actual biological nature, and hence what is good for it by nature. If porn in fact causes destruction of our biological nature, then like polluting toxins dumped into our air or water or ingested in our bodies, we can rightly call porn moral pollution, or more exactly, sexual pollution: the toxification of sexual desire.

Well, we've already gone through two kinds of real, measurable damage done by porn: chronic, widespread ED and addiction. ED kills the capacity for sexual intercourse, an essential part of our animal nature. Reminding us of the obvious, researcher Donald Hilton adds, "the powerful drives to eat and to procreate are successfully expressed in species that survive, and lines that do not reproduce with net-positive fertility rates, for whatever reason, become extinct. Regardless of how higher cortical function [in the brain] colors sex with other recreational nuances, evolutionary procreative pressures eventually trump purely recreational motives in biologically successful species, including humans."[32] Are we courting extinction? That's a serious question.

---

[32] Donald Hilton, Jr., "Pornography addiction—a supranormal stimulus considered in the context of neuroplasticity," *Socioaffective Neuroscience & Psychology* 3 (July 2013): 1–6. Quote from p. 1.

Further, it should be equally obvious that addiction destroys the capacity for free choice, an essential part of our human nature. "Virtually every study on addiction has demonstrated atrophy of multiple areas of the brain," notes Hilton, "particularly those associated with frontal volitional control and the reward-salience centers."[33] Addiction, continues Hilton, "can be described as disordered salience," that is, a disorder of what draws our attention in the environment. "Instead of wanting that which will enhance survival [as occurs with natural salience-directed activity], the addicted are motivated to want even when it is clearly harmful. . . ."[34] In other words, sexual addiction is slavery to the self-destruction of our own sexual nature: it kills our capacity to choose anything sexually except porn.

But other aspects of porn's polluting effects have surfaced. The extent of these problems has brought together on the Internet one of the greatest pools of experimental subjects ever gathered: the porn-addicted who, especially because of ED but also because of a host of other deleterious symptoms, reveal more ill effects of porn they've suffered, as well as the exhilarating effects of detoxification (that is, giving it up).[35]

The same set of symptoms arise again and again: along with ED, irritability, fatigue, sleeplessness, trembling, inability to focus or concentrate, depression, completely

---

[33] Ibid., 3.

[34] Ibid., 3. See also Andreas G. Philaretou, Ahmed Y. Mahfouz, and Katherine R. Allen, "Use of Internet Pornography and Men's Well-Being," *International Journal of Men's Health* 4, no. 2 (Summer 2005): 149–169.

[35] There is a host of websites devoted to recovery from porn, most significantly yourbrainonporn.com, Reddit/NoFap, Reboot Nation, Reddit/PornFree, YourBrainRebalanced, and NoFap.org.

deadened sexual desire for an actual person of the opposite sex, completely dead libido, significant social awkwardness, loss of job or flunking in school, development of ever more alarming sexual tastes, panic attacks, memory impairment, and thoughts of suicide. As the conversation among recovering porn addicts makes clear, they realized that the symptoms were porn-caused because the ill effects went away after they quit.[36]

While some of these ill effects may be due to the obsessive use of the Internet itself (as seen in Internet gaming addicts), it is the pornographic addiction that causes the obsessive use of the Internet, thereby compounding the damage. Obviously some of these symptoms are caused by the pornography itself, since they do not appear with Internet gaming addiction or non-pornographic Internet addiction.[37] Moreover, scientists have found that porn creates the highest incidence of Internet addiction.[38] The Internet makes it worse precisely because of the nature of the medium itself: it makes porn accessible, affordable, and anonymous,[39] thereby removing previous social, economic, and moral restraints that kept porn use under (relative)

---

[36] For a convenient gathering of the typical reports of recovered porn addicts see Wilson, *Your Brain on Porn*, chap. 1. On ill effects in college aged males see Michael Levin, Jason Lillis, and Steven C. Hayes, "When is Online Pornography Viewing Problematic Among College Males? Examining the Moderating Role of Experiential Avoidance," *Sexual Addiction & Compulsivity* 19 (2012): 168–180.

[37] On the damage done by Internet gaming addiction see Jung-Hye Kwon, Chung-Suk Chung, and Jung Lee, "The Effects of Escape from Self and Interpersonal Relationship on the Pathological Use of Internet Games," *Community Mental Health Journal* 47 (2011): 113–121.

[38] Gert-Jan Meerkerk, Regina J. J. M. Van Den Eijnden, and Henk F. L. Garretsen, "Predicting Compulsive Internet Use: It's All about Sex!" *CyberPsychology & Behavior* 9, no. 1 (2006): 95–103.

[39] Ibid., 101.

control in the past. So, we've managed to yoke together the destructive effects of two addictions, porn addiction and Internet addiction, thereby creating a doubly toxic effect.[40]

And you will not be surprised that porn kills romance, warping all of the wonderful and even more intricate aspects of our human biology we outlined above that so beautifully bring romance to its consummation in the feast of marriage. We've noted the hijacking of dopamine and the reward system, but porn does the same to testosterone and norepinephrine, funneling the sexual anticipation and focus they provide on the pornographic images on the screen, with norepinephrine burning the images that initiated the arousal into the memory of the porn addicted. The flood of dopamine and the simultaneous shutting down of the amygdala at masturbatory climax mean that the euphoric pleasure and the complete shutdown of fear, anxiety, and anger are deeply fused with those ever more degrading pornographic images, rather than a real woman. And perhaps most perverse of all, oxytocin and vasopressin are released enhancing the great feeling of satisfaction, with vasopressin binding the man to the pornographic images.[41] He binds himself to porn, and porn binds him

---

[40] On the ill effects of Internet addiction itself, whatever the source, see Matthias Brand, "Prefrontal control and Internet addiction: a theoretical model and review of neuropsychological and neuroimaging findings," *Frontiers in Human Neuroscience* 8 (May 2014): 1–13.

[41] See the excellent account in William Struthers, *Wired for Intimacy*, chap. 4. See also Larry Young, "The Neural Basis of Pair Bonding in a Monogamous Species: A Model for Understanding the Biological Basis of Human Behavior," in *Offspring: Human Fertility Behavior in Biodemographic Perspective*, https://www.ncbi.nlm.nih.gov/books/NBK97287/#_ch4_s4; and Thomas Insel, "The Challenge of Translation in Social Neuroscience: A Review of Oxytocin, Vasopressin, and Affiliative Behavior," *Neuron* 65 (March 25, 2010): 768–779.

in addiction. Since the addiction causes tolerance, he is binding himself, biologically, to the ever more horrifying, unnatural, and violent images of the rape, torture, choking, and utter humiliation of women.

It isn't difficult to see how all of this would destroy both romance and marriage because more and more men, married or unmarried, care less and less about having sex with actual women. In one study, done in Japan, almost 40 percent of men between the ages of 16–19 had no interest in sex with actual women. Likewise, in men between the ages of 20–24, and 45–49, about 22 percent had no interest in sex with actual women. Another study found about 20 percent of younger men in France had no sexual interest in actual women.[42] The reason? Porn. Actual women don't compare with those on the screen, either in what they look like or in what they are willing to do. It doesn't take much to figure out that porn would wreck marriages. The American Academy of Matrimonial Lawyers, the top 1,600 lawyers dealing with divorce, report that 56 percent of divorces they deal with are the result of a spouse's obsession with porn.[43] If human marital love is the perfection of our sexual nature, then this is a decidedly destructive and unnatural result.

And what of the young in our porn-saturated society? With smartphones and computers, they have access to porn earlier and earlier—the average age currently is

---

[42] Cited in Wilson, 43.

[43] Cited in *The Impact of Internet Pornography on Marriage and the Family: A Review of the Research,* 14 (2005) (testimony of Jill C. Manning, M.S.), available at http://s3.amazonaws.com/thf_media/2010/pdf/ManningTST. pdf. See also Kevin B. Skinner, Ph.D., "Is Porn Really Destroying 500,000 Marriages Annually?" *Psychology Today* (December 12, 2011), https:// www.psychologytoday.com/blog/inside-porn-addiction/201112/ is-porn-really-destroying-500000-marriages-annually.

about thirteen–fourteen years old but too often occurs much earlier. Studies have shown what should be obvious anyway: that frequent viewing of sexually explicit material by teenagers results in engaging in more casual sexual encounters, in lowering the age of first intercourse, in less satisfaction with romantic relationships, and in much greater desire to engage in the kinds of unnatural sexual practices portrayed in hardcore porn.[44] How could rape porn not create date rape? Thus, porn toxifies youth as well.

Porn and Human Trafficking

The Left often prides itself on being historically against slavery and being for sexual liberation. The ironic truth is that porn, the great product of sexual liberation, is also the chief cause of human sexual trafficking, the slavery of our time.

But I stress again—given the common notion that porn is a private thing—that porn has destructive social effects as well. I mentioned the increased damage to marriages, and failed marriages have enormous socio-economic effects. That's all bad enough. But even more horrible, porn contributes to human trafficking, the reintroduction of sexual slavery, where young (and ever-younger) girls are either

---

[44] See Elizabeth Morgan, "Associations between Young Adults' Use of Sexually Explicit Materials and Their Sexual Preferences, Behaviors, and Satisfaction," *Journal of Sex Research* 48, no. 6 (2011): 520–530; and Gert Martin Hald, Lisette Kuyper, Philippe C. G. Adam, and John B. F. de Wit, "Does Viewing Explain Doing? Assessing the Association between Sexually Explicit Materials Use and Sexual Behaviors in a Large Sample of Dutch Adolescents and Young Adults," *Journal of Sexual Medicine* 10 (2013): 2986–2995.

kidnapped or tricked into becoming slaves who must do *anything* and *everything* the johns demand—and much of what they want is defined by their immersion in hardcore pornography.[45] Porn now drives prostitution, not just in regard to increasing demand, but also in increasing supply. And that's where human trafficking comes in.

When I first started reading about sexual trafficking in Victor Malarak's *The Natashas*, I felt, quite literally, sick to my stomach and had trouble sleeping for some time.[46] Teenage girls in poor countries, wanting to help support their families or desperate for a better life, are lured by ads promising a better life working in the hotel industry, or as a nanny, or in the fashion industry in sparkling First World countries. They show up at the appointed time and are kidnapped—stuffed in cars and driven across borders to remote "collection centers," where "hundreds of women are held captive in the basements, cellars and attics, awaiting their turn on the auction block." At these "sex slave auctions," the "girls appear naked on stage with numbers in their hands."[47]

Sex-slave traders make a lot of money. As Malarak notes, "Pimps often brag that a woman purchased for $1500 can bring in $100 an hour . . . making back their investment in just a few nights."[48] Amazing profits draw those who are eager to make big money. European com-

---

[45] David E. Guinn and Julie DiCaro, *Pornography: Driving the Demand in International Sex Trafficking* (Los Angeles: Captive Daughters Media, 2007).

[46] At the very least, one should read Victor Malarek's *The Natashas: Inside the New Global Sex Trade* (New York: Arcade, 2004); and David Batstone, *Not for Sale: The Return of the Global Slave Trade—and How We Can Fight It* (New York: Harper, 2010).

[47] Malarek, 37.

[48] Ibid., 46.

missioner Anna Diamantopoulou, who studies trafficking, reports that sex trafficking

> is a booming industry, run with ruthless efficiency by powerful, multinational criminal networks. . . . There are not casual criminals. They run well-funded, well-organized, influential organizations. They know their business inside out and respond to changes in the market with a speed unmatched by even the most competitive corporations. Their expertise and their ability to exploit the market are surpassed only by their disregard for human life. Women are bought, sold and hired out like any other product. The bottom line is profit.[49]

As one European trafficker boasted, if you want sex slaves, it is "No problem. The price is $10,000 with the girl landed [i.e., flown in to location]. It is simple. It is easy to get access to the girls. It's a phone call. I know the brokers in Moscow, St. Petersburg and Kyiv. I can call Moscow tomorrow and show you how easy it is. I can get ten to fifteen girls shipped to me in a week."[50]

Once bought by the pimps, these most vile of men physically and morally "break the girls in." They force them to watch X-rated movies of the kind I've described above, so they can learn what is expected of them. The men-scum rape the girls, force them to have anal and oral sex, and teach them the importance of groaning in feigned pleasure with every painful humiliation. If they object, they will either be beaten, or one of the girls will be

---

[49] Quoted in Malarek, 46.
[50] Quoted in Malarek, 54.

killed so the rest learn what's in store for those unwilling to obey. They must turn ten to twenty tricks a night, and turn over all the money. They sleep on dirty mattresses at the brothel. If they try to escape, they are killed, or (as promised) one of their family members is killed. They not only must act out, multiple times every night, the most degraded fantasies of those who've watched porn, but are often taken to "act" in porn.

Prostitutes are often victims of abuse as young children, and begin "work" on average at about thirteen years old. They work in a climate of ever-present violence, from brutal beatings, to rape, and even death (with a mortality rate of forty times the average).[51] As one prostitute in America confided, "I was beaten with 2 x 4 boards, I had my fingers and toes broken by a pimp, and I was raped more than 30 times."[52]

Those who glamorize prostitution, or who push for legalization as a way to sanitize it, don't understand the real, brutal world of prostitution. As Melissa Farley (who has studied it) shows, prostitutes exhibit all the symptoms of post-traumatic stress syndrome (PTSS), and prostitutes report that working under legalized prostitution is worse than working on the streets.[53]

There is no doubt that Internet pornography, especially as it becomes more and more toxic, fuels prostitution. As Victor Malarak, who has studied sexual trafficking and

---

[51] For the relationship of violence to prostitution, see Melissa Farley, Isin Baral, Merab Kiremire, and Ufuk Sezgin, "Prostitution in Five Countries: Violence and Post Traumatic Stress Disorder," *Feminism & Psychology* 8, no. 4 (1988): 405–426.

[52] Ibid., 408.

[53] Ibid., 421. See also Melissa Farley, *Prostitution, Trafficking, and Traumatic Stress* (New York: Routledge, 2004).

pornography in detail, has aptly stated, "the net has become the biggest whorehouse on the planet,"[54] and an absolute boon to the global sex-slave prostitution industry.

So, you on the Left. Isn't sexual slavery enough to warrant calling porn a kind of moral pollution? What else do we have to add for us to call it morally evil? Isn't it, if anything, even more horribly toxic than what we find in our landfills?

Just as we should not let the Right say "out of sight, out of mind" in regard to all the trash we're producing, the Left can't pretend any longer that porn is just a private affair, "out of sight, out of mind." There's too much sexual garbage being produced. We must admit, then, that just like our air, just like our land, just like our oceans and streams, just like our own bodies, we can pollute our natural sexuality, degrading and deforming our own sexual nature almost beyond recognition (although one hopes not beyond repair).

What would that repair look like? As with all changing from a vice to a virtue, it is difficult to break deeply engrained bad habits, but bad habits are only cured by doing the opposite, in this case, by refraining completely from porn and aiming our sexuality back to its proper natural goal. The proper sexual virtue is chastity, a sub-virtue of temperance, the virtue that deals with moderating all pleasurable human activities and guiding them to their natural fulfillment.

In this regard, it's instructive to hear the testimonies of previously porn-addicted husbands about what happened when they gave porn up. One fifty-year-old recovering porn addict confessed, "I was always comparing the porn

---

[54] Malarek, 80.

scenarios with my real life and real wife and feeling dis-
satisfied. Now, things are shifting. During intercourse
last night, I felt suddenly very intimate, almost scarily intimate, deep contact I have never experienced before. It
felt kind of shocking to me. It was wonderful in a way I
can't describe, but I am in kind of awe over it."[55]

Another happily reports that after two hundred days
porn-free, "I now have an undeniable sex drive. I want my
wife more than ever. If a long time passes without sex, I
feel this thing called 'sexual tension,' which is apparently real. I notice things I never noticed [about my wife]
before. Hair tossing, quick glances, breathing patterns,
body language. It is a different world."[56] Indeed.

Yet another recovering husband tells us that "Now,
almost 8 months after quitting porn, I'm finding that the
[porn-driven] fantasies I used to have don't appeal to me
anymore . . . at all. What I found is that my wife and I
both enjoy sex much, much more when there is no fantasy
involved; just the two of us in the moment."[57]

And finally, one unmarried man, off porn for three
months, noted, "My bad habit of seeing only the beauty in
women automatically shifted. Right now I want to go out
there and find a mate. My sexual desire has never been
higher, and I'm more observant towards women who could
become good girlfriends and eventually mothers. It's not
entirely about beauty anymore."[58]

But of course, cleaning up the pollution of porn is not
just an individual endeavor. Just as we've got society-wide

---

[55] Wilson, 47–49.
[56] Ibid.
[57] Ibid.
[58] Ibid.

garbage pollution and obesity which we must transform socially and culturally, so also we cannot recover from porn unless we transform ourselves socially and culturally in regard to our sexuality.

Sex is, paradoxically, the most private and intimate of acts, but one which (as we can see from porn) affects all of society. Ironically, we have turned this truth upside down—and here, the Left is squarely to blame—by making sex an ever more *public* act through the ever-increasing sexualization and pornographization of society, even while claiming the right to sexual liberation and pornography under the guise of the right to *privacy*. Why, we must ask, do we think we have a right to pollute our sexuality through the private consumption of pornography any more than we have a right, in the name of privacy, to the consumption that brings us piles of garbage?

CHAPTER SIX

The Global Warming Debate

Why Look at Global Warming?

For obvious reasons, in a book about the environment, we've got to address *the* hot-button controversy, global warming. Recalling the previous overgeneralizations about the Left and the Right, things are pretty predictable in regard to this issue.

The Left is convinced that global warming is happening and, if ignored, will lead to unprecedented peril; therefore, immediate and decisive international action is necessary. Moreover, the Left believes that any scientific evidence brought up against global warming is ideology masquerading as science, the intellectual equivalent of Young Earth Creationists, except funded by the big oil companies.

The Right is convinced that global warming is not happening, and that there is significant scientific evidence calling global warming into question. Moreover, the Right tends to see the whole thing as a Left-wing, pseudo-scientific scam brewed up in order to commandeer political power to ram through radical environmentalism's pet projects. Therefore, the brouhaha will soon enough blow over if it's ignored or ridiculed or, best of all, scientifically disproven.

So, we don't seem to be getting anywhere in regard to our public debates about global warming. That's one very good reason to address the issue in this book about catholic ecology. We've got to sort this out in a way that avoids the bitterness of the debate.

But that's not the only reason the issue has got to be addressed in this book about the catholic understanding of ecology written by me, a Catholic. Pope Francis addressed global warming in his environmental encyclical, *Laudato si'*, throwing his weight behind those who believe global warming is real and a serious issue that demands immediate attention. In his words,

> A very solid scientific consensus indicates that we are presently witnessing a disturbing warming of the climatic system. In recent decades this warming has been accompanied by a constant rise in the sea level and, it would appear, by an increase of extreme weather events, even if a scientifically determinable cause cannot be assigned to each particular phenomenon. Humanity is called to recognize the need for changes of lifestyle, production and consumption, in order to combat this warming or at least the human causes which produce or aggravate it. . . .
>
> There is an urgent need to develop policies so that, in the next few years, the emission of carbon dioxide and other highly polluting gases can be drastically reduced, for example, substituting for fossil fuels and developing sources of renewable energy.[1]

---

[1]   *Laudato si'*, §§23, 26.

If you read the headlines and stories when the encyclical was released you might have thought that the entire encyclical was about global warming. The truth is that the pope said very little about global warming or climate change (it is mentioned in just four out of two-hundred-forty-six paragraphs). With the media ever ready to kick up a storm over a sound bite, rather than facilitate cool analysis of the entire encyclical, the rest of the encyclical (about 98 percent) got lost in the swirl of dust created by the media whipping up passions on both sides.

Again, the reaction to *Laudato si'* by the Left and Right was predictable, as well as amusing and instructive. It was amusing and instructive because, as the quote suggests, the pope certainly seemed to side with the Left about the significant dangers of global warming/climate change. Suddenly the Left was enamored with Catholic claims of papal infallibility! "The Pope has spoken!" they trumpeted.

True, but the pope has spoken about a lot of other issues—abortion, pornography, the sanctity of heterosexual monogamous marriage, the male priesthood, the divinity of Jesus Christ, the reality of the Holy Spirit guiding the Catholic Church, etc., all of which the Left generally rejects.

The pope is not a partisan, however. He speaks on behalf of both natural *and* moral ecology, the whole Catholic deal, the order of creation and redemption. You can't cherry pick your infallibility. Furthermore—and even more instructive—the infallibility of the pope is limited to when "he proclaims by a definitive act a doctrine pertaining to faith or morals,"[2] that is, about the very

---

[2] Second Vatican Council, Dogmatic Constitution on the Church *Lumen gentium* (November 21, 1964), §25; *Catechism of the Catholic Church*, 891.

things that the Left, by and large, ignores. His statements about global warming/climate change *must be taken with the utmost seriousness by the faithful* because he, as the pope, has made them in his considered judgment in an encyclical, *but he was not declaring an infallible doctrine.*

The Right, while generally affirming his authority in regard to moral matters and theological doctrines (more or less, depending on whether one is Catholic or Protestant), did *not* want to hear the pope say anything at all in favor of the Left's most adamantly passionate environmental issue, because it seemed to give papal approval for what they deemed to be pseudo-science and what they fear would happen if even greater power and economic resources were handed over to the federal government or the United Nations to "fix" the problem. The Right, so ready to affirm the pope's moral authority in regard to sexual morality, was signaling barely suppressed rumbles of Sedevacantism (from the Latin, *sede vacante*, denoting those who hold that the pope is no true pope, and hence the seat of St. Peter is vacant).

Both sides are wrong, because they are each taking half-truths for whole truths. We've got to take seriously the whole catholic ecological understanding, both environmental and moral (as the Catholic Church does). That means—because the pope has spoken about global warming, and given his considered opinion—Catholics have got to take global warming seriously.

But so does everyone else, Left or Right. Maybe it really is happening, and the Left is correct. Or maybe it's not, and the Left is wrong. Maybe it is based upon stellar science, and the Right is wrong. Or maybe it's based upon pseudo-science, and the Right is right. The only way to find out is (drumroll) to study the issue in depth, and look not at a partisan part, but at the big picture—very big, as it turns out. We need to look at global warming from the cosmic perspective, a vantage point that has the advantage of shaking us loose from our parochial obsession with merely looking at things from the perspective of Earth.

My goal in this chapter is not to settle the debate, but to widen and deepen it considerably, bringing a more comprehensive and interesting perspective on the issue which should surprise and enlighten both the Left and Right. And we're about to go as wide as it gets, back to the beginning of the universe. Of course, I'm providing an overview from this greatly expanded vantage point, so I will try to avoid overburdening readers with too many technical details. For those who are interested, however, I've included scientific and philosophical detail in the footnotes.

Global Warming and the Goldilocks Principle

The whole debate about global warming seems to boil down to one thing, the amount of carbon dioxide in our atmosphere (the Left asserting that too much human-produced carbon dioxide will cause dramatic and destructive increases in Earth's temperature which will have deleterious, even catastrophic effects).

The presence of this infamous greenhouse gas, CO_2, in the right amount (not too little, not too much, but *just right*), is part of the delicate balance that makes Earth a habitable planet for complex life. Too little CO_2 would mean an Earth that's too cold for us, and too much would yield an uninhabitable hothouse.

But this kind of delicate balance isn't confined to the amount of CO_2 in Earth's atmosphere. It's a common principle in nature, and so it has received a name. This "just-rightness," wherever it exists, has been called the Goldilocks Principle.[3] The condition of "just-rightness" means that if something throws off the balance anywhere along the line, then life itself becomes impossible.

Again, global warming enthusiasts argue that we're throwing the just-rightness of our atmosphere off by our increased production of CO_2. This is important to understand because sometimes, in the heat of the debate about global warming, it may seem that CO_2 is some kind of an evil pollutant. Such is not the case, and calling it a pollutant is gravely misleading. That term should be reserved for the kind of pollution that China is now experiencing, where breathing the air is the equivalent of smoking two packs of cigarettes a day.[4] The issue is the right amount of CO_2 in the atmosphere—not too much, not too little—as will become clear if we look at things in more detail.

Obviously, the Sun is the original source of Earth's warmth, but it's not enough. We need an atmosphere. If we subtracted our atmosphere, so that the Sun was the only cause of our warmth, we'd have a mean global temperature range somewhere between -7 to +1° F (at mid-latitudes)—cold enough to freeze our oceans.[5] You

---

[3]   The Goldilocks Principle is usually associated with the "just right" conditions of the early universe, but it also fits well the "just right" conditions of Earth. See, for example, Paul Davies, *The Goldilocks Enigma: Why Is the Universe Just Right for Life?* (Boston: Houghton Mifflin, 2006).

[4]   Robert Rohde and Richard Muller, "Air Pollution in China: Mapping of Concentrations and Sources," *Berkeley Earth*, http://berkeleyearth.org/wp-content/uploads/2015/08/China-Air-Quality-Paper-July-2015.pdf.

[5]   Calculations of temperature range fall within the named spectrum. See Jonathan Lunine, *Astrobiology* (San Francisco, CA: Addison Wesley,

want an atmosphere, complete with CO_2. Subtract it, and Earth would be summarily popsicled.

It's our atmosphere, then, that brings Earth's temperature up to what's called the "habitable range," the range of temperatures wherein it's warm enough to have the large bodies of *liquid* water essential for life, but not so warm that the water bodies boil away.

What keeps it within that small temperature range is Earth's atmospheric "greenhouse." Much like the windows of a greenhouse, which let in visible light and then trap the reradiated heat, the chemical constitution of our atmosphere readily lets in the visible light wavelength of the electromagnetic spectrum provided by the Sun. That sunlight becomes absorbed at the surface of Earth and then is reradiated as heat, that is, as infrared radiation in the electromagnetic spectrum.

But that heat doesn't just all leak out into space again; instead, it is "trapped," or absorbed, in our atmosphere by CO_2 and the other greenhouse gases, water vapor (H_2O), methane (CH_4), nitrous oxide (N_2O), and ozone (O_3). Without these gases in the atmosphere (water vapor and carbon dioxide doing the bulk of the warming), we wouldn't have a lush greenhouse on Earth, but a lifeless icehouse. Far from being evil pollutants, these greenhouse gases make our Earth's temperature not too cold, not too hot, but just right.

2005), 337; and Charles Langmuir and Wally Broecker, *How to Build a Habitable Planet: The Story from the Big Bang to Humankind*, revised and expanded (Princeton, NJ: Princeton University Press, 2012), 266–267, esp. table 9-2.

Goldilocks at the Very Beginning: How We Even Got CO_2

But this just-rightness isn't confined to our present atmosphere; it's a principle we see throughout nature. Indeed, the fact that there *is* carbon and oxygen at all—both absolutely necessary for life, and united in CO_2 in our atmosphere—is the result of extraordinary just-rightness in the production of these elements in our early universe.[6] In fact, the term "Goldilocks Principle" was first coined in regard to the original just-rightness at our cosmic beginning.[7] Nowhere is this clearer than in the cosmic

---

[6] On the fine-tuning entailed in the stellar production of carbon and oxygen see John Barrow and Frank Tipler, *The Anthropic Cosmological Principle* (Oxford and New York: Oxford University Press, 1986), 243–255; Neil Manson, ed., *God and Design: the Teleological Argument and Modern Science* (London and New York: Routledge, 2003), chap. 9; John Barrow, ed., *Fitness of the Cosmos for Life: Biochemistry and Fine-Tuning* (Cambridge, UK: Cambridge University Press, 2008), 20–30; my *Meaningful World: How the Arts and Sciences Reveal the Genius of Nature* (Downers Grove, IL: InterVarsity Press, 2006), chap. 6; and Michael Denton, *Nature's Destiny: How the Laws of Biology Reveal Purpose in the Universe* (New York: Free Press, 1998), chap. 5.

[7] Again, see Paul Davies, *The Goldilocks Enigma*. For those interested in going deeper, I offer the following as examples. There would be no stars to cook heavier elements, like carbon and oxygen, if there had been too much expansion energy (or too little gravity) in the Big Bang because too much energy would blow things out with such force that no stars could form (too little gravity would have the same result, since the gravitational pull allows for matter to cluster into stars). Conversely, too little expansion energy (or too much gravity) would mean the Big Bang would immediately collapse on itself in a so-called Big Crunch, the result again being that carbon and oxygen would not have been produced. As Cambridge Astronomer Royal Martin Rees has said, the "required precision" for this exceedingly tight fine-tuning of energy and matter necessary for the proper rate of expansion "is astonishing," so much so that the balance "one second after the Big Bang" could not have differed "by more than one part in a million billion (one in 10^{15}) . . ." (Martin Rees, *Just Six Numbers: the Deep Forces that Shape the Universe* [New York: Basic Books, 2000], 99).

production of CO_2. (Readers, bear with me for a bit of technical information, because it will have significant implications for the debate about global warming.)

The Big Bang gave us the first, simplest elements—hydrogen and helium—but the development of the "heavier" elements like carbon and oxygen occurred many tens of millions of years later because heavier element formation had to wait for the development and subsequent burning down of the first stars, made of hydrogen and helium. The immense pressures and temperatures available in slow-burning stars fused the lighter elements together to make heavier ones. Such star-burning created carbon from helium and beryllium, and oxygen from carbon and helium.[8]

Similarly, atoms themselves are rather complex, consisting of positively-charged protons in the center, and negatively charged electrons in surrounding orbits. As we've all learned in our Introduction to Chemistry classes, atoms differ by the number of protons in their nucleus, beginning with Hydrogen which has one. Carbon has six protons and oxygen eight. What forces the positively-charged protons in elements beyond hydrogen together? Why don't they repel each other, like positive ends of magnets? The answer is that repulsion is overcome by the strong nuclear force. If the strong force was just a bit weaker (by a mere one-half of one percent), it would severely unbalance the rate of carbon and oxygen production, and the universe would be unfit for life. A little weaker still, and no atoms greater than hydrogen could form—again, no life. The same fine-tuning pertains to the electromagnetic force: change it a bit, and we don't get carbon and oxygen. Ditto with the mass of the neutron, as compared to the mass of the proton. See Barrow and Tipler, *The Anthropic Cosmological Principle*, 326–327; Manson, *God and Design*, 182–195.

[8] To be more exact chemically, these first stars burned hydrogen to form helium. When the star then contracts, temperature increases and helium atoms can be fused to form beryllium (4He + 4He → 8Be), then beryllium and helium can be fused to make carbon (8Be + 4He →12C), and finally, we have carbon and helium producing oxygen (12C + 4He →16O). For a more detailed account, but still accessible to the diligent layperson, see Jonathan Lunine, *Astrobiology* (San Francisco, CA:

All of this had to be just right before stars could create carbon from helium and beryllium, and oxygen from carbon and helium, the result being that we could (eventually) have CO_2—and hence the possibility of arguing over global warming.

Yet, right here, scientists have discovered things were even more amazingly precise. The creation of carbon and oxygen out of lesser elements wasn't just a matter of simple mathematical addition. It had to be very, very precisely rigged. As astronomer Fred Hoyle famously realized, if there were not some very special conditions pertaining to the cooking of these two elements, first carbon, and then oxygen, the stars never could have produced the abundance of carbon and oxygen we know the universe actually has, the abundance which has allowed for life on Earth.

Hoyle conjectured that there must have been exceedingly precise nuclear "resonance" states in carbon and oxygen (resonance being the amplification of energy when waves from two sources precisely match[9]). It turned out he was right in his prediction, as further investigation confirmed. As astronomer Owen Gingerich explains, "Had the resonance level in the carbon been 4 percent lower, there would be essentially no carbon. Had the level in the oxygen been only a half percent higher, virtually all of the carbon would have been converted to oxygen."[10] While

---

Addison Wesley, 2005), sections 5.3–4. For a later technical affirmation of Hoyle's work, which lessens the anthropic significance somewhat, see M. Livio, D. Hollowell, A. Weiss, and J. W. Truran, "The anthropic significance of the existence of an excited state of 12C," *Nature* 340 (July 1989): 281–284.

[9] A clear account of nuclear resonance in relation to the production of carbon can be found in Davis, 135–139.

[10] Owen Gingerich, "Revisiting *The Fitness of the Environment*," in John Barrow, ed., *Fitness of the Cosmos for Life*, 28–29.

oxygen is wonderful and essential for life, you've also got to have carbon as well.

In regard to these weird "coincidences" that allowed it all to occur, Fred Hoyle famously noted that, "A commonsense interpretation of the facts suggests that a superintellect has monkeyed with physics, as well as with chemistry and biology, and that there are no blind forces worth speaking about in nature. The numbers one calculates from the facts seem to me so overwhelming as to put this conclusion beyond question."[11] To Hoyle, and many others, *the precision seemed to have significant theistic implications* (which readers may wish to follow in the material I've included in the footnotes).

So, here's one very good reason for the Right to take the possibility of global warming seriously. What if studying the intricate and delicate balance of CO_2 in our atmosphere, and what might upset it, was part of a larger scientific analysis of such just-rightness that leads to God? Certainly, from the perspective of the Judeo-Christian view, learning what amazing just-rightness sustains life on Earth should make us far more grateful for this great gift of life.

---

[11] Fred Hoyle, "The Universe: Past and Present Reflection," *Engineering & Science* (November 1981): 8–12. Hoyle was not just referring to the "coincidences" around the carbon atom, but also the fact that the vastly complicated systems of biology rest on the precise order of chemical structures in biomolecules, like DNA and enzymes, which would make production of these structures by random associations impossible. "I was constantly plagued [in my research] by the thought that the number of ways in which even a single enzyme could be wrongly constructed was greater than the number of all the atoms in the universe. So try as I would, I couldn't convince myself that even the whole universe would be sufficient to find life by random processes—by what are called the blind forces of nature." The only rational alternative being that "the origin of life was a deliberate intellectual act" (Ibid.).

Yet, it seems a part of our very human nature not to appreciate our home until we go away and realize how good we have it. This is certainly true about our home planet Earth, which will become even clearer if we take a tour of some other planets close by, a tour that will also help to emphasize what the Left is so concerned to avoid— becoming Venus.

A Quick Tour of Our Solar System

For all the fuss being made about it, the amount of CO_2 in Earth's atmosphere is amazingly small, about .04 percent. Not 4 percent, but four-one-hundredths of one percent.[12] Just for comparison, 96 percent of the atmosphere of Venus and 95 percent of Mars consists of carbon dioxide. Interesting facts given that these are Earth's closest planetary neighbors, Venus on the Sun side, and Mars on our outer side, and neither of these planets is habitable.

The Left is worried about us becoming Venus. Although Mercury is closer to the Sun than Venus, Venus is the hottest planet in the solar system, due in great part (you guessed it) to a very, very thick, heat-trapping CO_2 atmosphere. Travelers to this beautiful planet should expect daytime temperatures over 850° F. If we subtracted the thick shroud of CO_2 from Venus, the mean surface temperature would drop to about 130° F, which would put

---

[12] As I'll note later on, the amount has varied over time, from a high of 7,000 parts per million (or ppm) in the Cambrian period about 500 million years ago, to 180 ppm in our own "time," the so-called Quaternary Glaciation period of the last 2.5 million years. Scientists estimate CO_2 ppm levels have risen since the Industrial Revolution from about 300 to 400 ppm.

it within the temperature range of habitability, at least in the abstract.[13]

That's an interesting fact because Earth and Venus have about the same sum total amount of CO_2, counting both the CO_2 in the atmosphere and that which is locked up in the ground. The difference is that almost all of Venus's carbon dioxide resides in the atmosphere and almost all of Earth's resides in the ground.[14]

Venus is therefore an example of the "Runaway Greenhouse Effect" warned about by the most passionate global warming alarmists, an example of "too much-ness," rather than just-rightness.[15] But on the other side of Earth, we have the opposite situation with Mars.

For your trip to Mars, the most Earthlike planet in the solar system, you'll need a very good winter coat, as the average temperature is -80° F, with low temperatures of about -240° F at the poles. Temperature varies over a wide range even in one place, both seasonally and daily. Settle down on some of the milder real estate on the Red Planet, and you might experience a possible summer high just shy of 32° F, but a winter night might drop down to about -150° F. It's so cold on Mars that a significant portion of the at-

---

[13] Calculations from Langmuir and Broecker, 267, table 9-2.

[14] And so, as scientists Charles Langmuir and Wally Broecker point out, "Venus has the conditions that would prevail on Earth if all the CO_2 locked up in limestone and kerogen [on the earth] were to be released as CO_2 in the atmosphere." Kerogen refers to the organic chemical compounds in sedimentary rocks (276).

[15] We also know that Mercury, which is about halfway between Venus and the Sun, is actually a bit cooler precisely because it has essentially no atmosphere, and that lack of atmosphere causes wide temperature swings between day (800° F) and night (-280° F), with an average of about 333° F. By contrast, Earth's average temperature is just shy of a balmy 60° F. It's our atmosphere that keeps Earth from such wide and deadly temperature swings.

mospheric CO_2 condenses into dry ice in the winter. The result: no liquid water, no life.

Why so cold on Mars, given that the percentage of CO_2 is nearly the same as Venus's? Even though it's got plenty of CO_2, the atmosphere of Mars is about a hundred times thinner than Earth's, and it's also too far from the Sun. Thin atmospheres neither absorb nor retain solar radiation. So while part of the just-rightness of Earth consists in its precise distance from the Sun, it also has the right density of its atmosphere.[16]

Makes you appreciate your own home a bit more, I hope. The overall lesson in our tour is that the right amount of CO_2 in the atmosphere is essential, but we must add that it's only a small part of what keeps Earth within the habitable range of temperature. There's a whole lot more to the just-rightness that makes Earth a habitable home.

---

[16] Since Mars is the most Earth-like planet, we might well wonder what happened to its atmosphere. Mars is smaller than Earth and also has a lesser mass, both of which keep it from holding an atmosphere. Earth, being larger and denser, has a greater gravitational pull on its atmosphere, thereby keeping it from "floating" away. But that interesting difference is less important than the very strange and wonderful fact that Earth has a magnetic shield (magnetosphere) which deflects harmful charged particles released from the Sun called the solar wind—the wind that stripped the unprotected atmosphere of Mars away. Interestingly enough, Earth has the largest magnetic field of any of the terrestrial planets (i.e., Mercury, Venus, Earth, and Mars). While we're talking about the possible harmful effects from the Sun, we should add that the ozone (O_3) in our atmosphere is not only a greenhouse gas, but absorbs much of the potentially harmful ultraviolet light radiated from the Sun. To buttress all of these considerations, we might also look at the Moon. On the moon, you'll find almost no atmosphere, and hence, no thermostatic heat regulation. The result is temperatures vaulting as high as 260° F in the day and sinking to -280° F at night. (Those who live in desert regions experience a mini-lesson in this regard, since the desert atmosphere is less dense—very hot days, very cool nights.)

The Importance of a Good Roof (with Clouds)

One thing we've got over being in an actual greenhouse is the size of our atmosphere. Earth's atmospheric "roof" is way, way higher. That's part of what keeps us from turning into Venus.

Air near the surface of Earth is denser (i.e., has more molecules per volume) and so it can absorb more heat, while as we go further up in the atmosphere the air becomes thinner (i.e., has less molecules per volume). Despite what you've been told by Daedalus, it's actually colder as you fly upward toward the Sun.[17] When the air warms up significantly down near the surface of Earth, it rises upward, and the hotter air mixes with cooler, thereby moderating the overall temperature in Earth's atmospheric greenhouse.

Another part of what keeps Earth's temperature within the habitable range is cloud cover, another aspect of our "roof." When the Sun causes Earth to warm up, then we have more evaporation, and water is taken into the atmosphere, some of which becomes clouds. Since water vapor is actually a more important greenhouse gas than carbon dioxide, it would seem that an increase in temperature, which brings more water vapor into the atmosphere, would also lead to greater heat absorption, warming the planet further, even breaking away in a kind of runaway greenhouse effect (more warmth, more evaporation, more water vapor in the atmosphere, even more warmth, etc.). That is in fact what many on the Left worry about.

Why doesn't that happen? Clouds also deflect a significant portion of the incoming solar radiation, like, say,

---

[17] And, by the way, the fact that you can't breathe well at higher altitudes is caused by there being few oxygen molecules per volume of air.

"frosting" half of the glass panels in your greenhouse. The so-called "albedo effect" cools things down before they can heat up. (Snow likewise creates an albedo effect, reflecting sunlight, therefore leading to cooling.) The greater the cloud cover, the more of the Sun's incoming rays are deflected, something that is obvious to us when we feel the temperature difference if a cloud covers the Sun while we're out on a really hot day.

This is a rather ingenious "feedback" system. Excess heat causes evaporation, which increases cloud cover, thereby blocking more of the Sun's rays, and making things cool down again. A rather amazing roof! But the clouds above are a sign of yet another aspect of Earth's self-regulating temperature controls.

The Carbon Cycle and Earth's Thermostat

Those same clouds not only block Sun but bring rain, which removes both water vapor and carbon dioxide from the atmosphere, thereby reducing two key greenhouse gases in the atmosphere. What happens to all that washed-down CO_2?

Rain is actually made somewhat more acidic by the dissolving of atmospheric CO_2. But, happily, the slightly acidic rain helps to weather rocks, thereby releasing minerals, in particular, silicates. These now-available silicates bring about a chemical reaction with CO_2 that produces limestone, the result being a reduction of carbon dioxide and a cooling down of earth's thermostat.[18]

---

[18] To be more exact, available calcium silicate plus carbon dioxide yields limestone and silicone dioxide: $CaSiO_3 + CO_2 = CaCO_3 + SiO_2$.

As Harvard astronomer Owen Gingerich points out, this keeps Earth from being like Venus—smothered in atmospheric CO_2: "The earth's atmosphere would be similar [to Venus's] if the oceans [of Earth] had not dissolved the carbon dioxide and precipitated the excess in the form of limestone."[19] This part of the "carbon cycle" ensures that, unlike Venus, almost all of our carbon stays locked up in our crust, so we don't have a Venusian runaway Greenhouse.

Of course, cool-down means less evaporation and less weathering. Too much cooling down is not a good thing, however. Happily, the cooling allows a swing back to increasing CO_2, from exhalation by human beings and other breathers, but more importantly, from volcanoes. (In fact, if we did have a freeze over, our volcanoes would break through the ice and blow more CO_2 into the air, thereby breaking the cold spell via greenhouse gas emission.)[20]

The net result of this cycle is *homeostasis* (just like our bodies are homeostatic)—the maintenance of temperature equilibrium within a small range suitable for complex life.

So, while it may be controversial in the global warming debate whether the additional CO_2 emitted by the human burning of fossil fuels will overwhelm this carbon-silicate cycle, as well as any other negative feedbacks, what is not at issue is whether (independently of human beings) this cycle is ingeniously designed to achieve and maintain habitable temperatures on Earth.

In fact, there is another aspect of our wonderful planet that keeps us from turning into the Venus Hothouse—one

---

[19] Gingerich, 21. For more details on the carbon-silicate cycle see Lunine, *Astrobiology*, 344–348.
[20] Langmuir and Broecker, 278–280.

that, interestingly enough, proved to be a bit of an embarrassment for those asserting that Earth was in imminent endanger from overheating.

Global Warming Pause to Consider

If the Left is correct, we should be getting hotter, much hotter, because as all sides in the debate admit, over the last two decades, the amount of CO_2 in the atmosphere has increased from human causes. But during the same period, instead of things getting ever warmer, temperatures have flatlined—or to put it in terms of advocates of global warming, there has been a sustained "global warming pause."

One of the explanations given for the missing heat was that it is being absorbed by the oceans, which, while it may appear to be self-serving, is actually pointing to yet another amazing aspect of planet Earth and the marvelous properties of H_2O.

About 71 percent of Earth is covered with water—unlike any other known planet—and water as a compound has a suite of near-miraculous, anomalous properties, one of which is its extraordinarily high specific heat capacity in the liquid state. (Specific heat is the amount of heat required to raise the temperature of a substance 1° Celsius.) It's the ideal substance to absorb excessive heat, thereby significantly moderating Earth's surface temperatures.

Thus, when things start to heat up on Earth, the oceans absorb that heat and the increased heat also melts ice, thereby increasing the amount of surface liquid water that can absorb excess heat, as well as offering a larger surface area for evaporation (providing more cloud cover to deflect heat, and more rain to wash excess CO_2 out of the atmosphere). Happily, there are also ocean currents which, like the atmosphere, disperse the heated water around the globe, cooling off areas where the Sun is most intense and carrying the heated water to cooler areas.

So, it was perfectly rational for the Left to suggest that the "pause" in global warming was the result of the wonderful fact that Earth is covered with water, but this adds another very scientific factor that (along with the carbon cycle) calls into question the Left's view that our doom is imminent. Perhaps Earth's complex homeostatic system can take care of our increased CO_2 production, at least up to a point.

And that's not the end of it. There are even more amazing things keeping Earth within the habitable temperature range. Let's not forget the beneficial effect of the CO_2 eaters, a reason why the Right should consider going more green.

CO_2 Eaters and the Green Revolution: Light Becomes Life

We remind ourselves that carbon is not a villainous pollutant, but an essential life-giving substance. Since both land plants and phytoplankton on oceans use CO_2 for photosynthesis, they take carbon dioxide out of the atmosphere, release oxygen, and create, in themselves, the rich bottom of the food chain without which the more complex, energy-needy animals cannot exist.

An interesting illustration of the effectiveness of these CO_2 eaters is the enormous decrease in the amount of CO_2 in the atmosphere since photosynthesizing land plants came on the scene about half a billion years ago. Way back then, due to fuming and spouting volcanoes, Earth's atmosphere had much more CO_2, about 6,000–7,000 ppm (parts per million), as compared to our present-day levels of 400 ppm. The CO_2 ppm gradually came way down as plants spread and diversified over the globe (although one must point out that it has risen from about 280 ppm, the level prior to the Industrial Revolution in the nineteenth century).[21]

Greening up Earth has another beneficial effect in regard to global warming. It decreases the amount of the Sun's radiation that is converted to heat. Rather than heating up the surface of the planet, the visible light is instead absorbed by photosynthesis, and the carbon is changed into the plant itself: carbon becomes life; the greenhouse gas becomes green. This botanical lushness is the energy-supplying foundation for all other forms of life; therefore, increased greening means increased diversity of herbivorous and carnivorous species, *and* it removes excess CO_2, transforming it into life-giving oxygen to boot.

Think about that, you on the Right. That's a very good reason to want more green and less concrete, more forests and less shopping malls. But it also makes clear that Earth's temperature-regulating system is far, far more complex than one is led to believe by thinking that CO_2 is the only factor we need to take into account. We shouldn't forget other factors, especially those that are even more obvious than Earth's luscious greenery, the Sun and its relation to Earth. First, the Sun.

---

[21] See Robert Carter, "The Scientific Context," in Alan Moran, ed., *Climate Change: The Facts* (Woodside, NH: Stockade Books, 2015), 70–71.

The Sun Enters the Debate about Climate Changes

Now in all this debate about global warming, it should occur to us that we're overlooking something. There is—oddly enough—a hidden element in the debate, the elephant in the solar system, so to speak, the Sun itself. Focusing the entire debate on the amount of CO_2 in the atmosphere deflects us from the obvious: *the source of warming is the Sun.* Without the Sun, there wouldn't be a debate.

But the Sun isn't just a big constantly streaming light bulb of a single, steady wattage. Granted, it's amazingly steady, but the Sun's intensity itself varies over time, to be precise, over eleven-year cycles. When there are more sunspots the intensity is greater (and Earth will be correspondingly warmer), when fewer, the intensity is less (and Earth will cool down).

All eleven-year cycles are not created equally, however. The minimum and maximum vary over time. Again, we have another non-human source of climate changes—temperature swings over time—and this must not be overlooked in our debates about global warming.

The following short history of climate change will illustrate why. The Sun seemed about "dead" between the years of AD 1650 and 1700, with almost no sunspots. There has been an increase in sunspot activity since then, reaching a peak at about the mid-twentieth century, but it's been *decreasing steadily since.*[22] During this period, Earth's temperatures have followed this increase and decrease in

---

[22] See "Yearly mean and monthly smoothed sunspot number," *Sunspot Index and Long-term Solar Observations,* http://www.sidc.be/silso/yearlyssnplot.

sunspot activity (which might lead us to suspect that the "pause" in global warming mentioned above could also have this, too, as a cause).

That "dead time" just mentioned above, between the years of 1650 and 1700, when so very little solar activity was occurring, is called a Maunder Minimum (after husband and wife astronomers E. Walter and Annie Maunder), a time when the number of sunspots at the low end of things is even lower than normal. It should be no surprise that this super-low period corresponds, historically, with the Little Ice Age, which lasted from about AD 1650 to 1850.[23]

Interestingly enough, the Sun's return to a more normal number of sunspots since 1850 and the increase in Earth's temperature correspond exactly with the increase in human-produced CO_2 during this period from 1850 to the present day. Moreover, for whatever reasons in the web of complexity that determines our climate, this particular warm period in the cycle from about 1850 onward has experienced an extremely moderate and stable climate.[24]

What does that mean for our ability to ferret out the exact contribution of human beings to global warming? Does it mean that increased CO_2 from human sources intensified the natural warming trend since the mid-1800s, or that temperature increases since 1850 alleged to have come from human-produced CO_2 are actually the result of overall increased sunspot activity? Or again, are human

---

[23] The lowest points of sunspot activity are actually reflected in the growth rate, or lack of it, in the rings of trees, when no sunspot activity occurred between about 1650–1720. See E. Kirsten Peters, *The Whole Story of Climate: What Science Reveals about the Nature of Endless Change* (Amherst, NY: Prometheus Books, 2012), chap. 6.

[24] See Langmuir and Broecker, 628–632.

contributions, in part, the cause of the moderate and stable climate we've experienced, or will the increasing CO_2 disturb that stability?

That all might be very difficult to settle. What is now scientifically beyond dispute—and hence, must enter the debate about global warming—is that sunspot activity oscillates over time, and correlates with temperatures on Earth. It is not all about the amount of CO_2 we're putting into the atmosphere.

A Disquieting Possibility?

This introduces a rather frightening possibility, one that global warming folk generally don't discuss. There has been a decrease in the number of sunspots in the solar cycles since 1950, and scientists are predicting that we are going to experience another Maunder Minimum in about fifteen years (2030), so that whatever else happens in the debate, it may very well be that the significantly decreased solar sunspots will ensure that we're about to enter a much colder temperature phase in our planet's history, perhaps another mini Ice Age.[25]

As I write this very paragraph, it has just been reported that the January 2016 sunspot activity is below normal, about the level it was during the so-called Dalton Minimum in the early 1800s that followed upon the previous Maunder Minimum just mentioned.[26]

---

[25] See "Irregular Heartbeat of the Sun Driven by Double Dynamo," *Royal Astronomical* (July 9, 2015), https://www.ras.org.uk/news-and-press/2680-irregular-heartbeat-of-the-sun-driven-by-double-dynamo.

[26] "Die Sonne im Januar 2016, Rekorde und Ozeanströmungen: Der Golf-strom bleibt stabil!" *Die kalte Sonne* (February 9, 2016), http://www.

Are we in for freezing rather than warming? That question will have to be settled by scientists who study the Sun and its relationship to Earth's temperature oscillations, and so must be part of the debate about the possibility of global warming. Now that we've looked at the effect of the Sun, we may turn to Earth's own contribution to climate change.

The Earth's Regular Irregularity and Climate Changes

Earth isn't just a stationary Big Blue Marble flying around the Sun in a nice, perfect circle. While its orbit is very close to circular, it is still elliptical; that is, there are still differences in the distance of Earth to Sun in its yearly orbit. When Earth is closer, more of the Sun's radiation hits Earth, and when further away, less.

Even here, however, things aren't exactly regular; that is, Earth doesn't always trace out the same ellipse around the Sun, but the ellipse varies over time—big time, in fact, in cycles of about 100,000 years, waxing and waning from being slightly more to slightly less elliptical, and back again. The more elliptical periods will cause greater seasonal contrasts on Earth for the obvious reason that when you flatten the circle more, the farther away swings on either end of the ellipse are from the Sun, while the flattened out parts of the orbit are closer to the Sun.

But that's not the only source of climate change in regard to Earth. As we all know, Earth also spins on its

---

kaltesonne.de/die-sonne-im-januar-2016-rekorde-und-ozeanstromungen-der-golfstrom-bleibt-stabil/.

axis (giving us night and day). Even more interesting is that we're also on a tilt in our axial spin, rather than spinning standing straight up, or perpendicular to our orbit around the Sun. All to the good, because that tilt gives us our seasons, as on a yearly basis we (in the Northern Hemisphere) tilt closer for summer, and away for winter.[27]

Here's some real just-rightness. Too much axial tilt would mean too much variation in the seasons; too little would mean that less of Earth was warmed and what was warmed would be much warmer. But as with our orbit, there's a bit of variability in the tilt, and that affects Earth's temperatures independently of what human beings do.

Earth's axial tilt deviates (or wobbles) just a bit from perfect regularity—not always tilted at 23.5° straight up, but moving back and forth from a tilt of 22.1° to 24.5°. That cycle takes 41,000 years. Since our seasons are determined by the tilt toward (summer) or away (winter) from the Sun, varying the tilt over these long stretches of time affects the severity or mildness of the seasons, with seasonal variations being less severe at 22.1° and more severe at 24.5°.

Now we've got to add the effects of the regularities and deviations in orbit and axial tilt together. A moment's thought leads us to ask: Do the effects line up or not? That is, do the variations in Earth's orbit every 100,000 years that affect the intensity of sunlight hitting Earth (called "solar insolation") have some connection to the effects of the variations in our tilt cycle every 41,000 years?

---

[27] We note that, among other things, the axial tilt helps spread heat more evenly over the surface, just as you might warm different parts of your body, standing in front of a fire, by turning it slightly to one side and the other and back again. These seasonal changes allow for a greater range of biodiversity over greater areas of Earth's surface.

The answer is yes, on cycles of about 21,000 years. The combined cyclical variations, even though quite small, do in fact have significant effects on Earth's climate during long-term intervals—called the Milankovitch effect after the astronomer Milutin Milanković, who first hypothesized it. If we look back over the last 800,000 years we find that greater periods of solar insolation (more intense sunlight) correspond to the reduction in Earth's ice sheets.[28]

Adding It All Up?

What does all this mean *for us?* The only way we can find out is to add it all together; that is, we need to take into account *all* of the factors that affect Earth's habitable temperature range, not just what human beings contribute. We have temperature variations throughout Earth's history. The temperature of Earth oscillates, and warming-up spikes in Earth's temperature are as normal as cooling down periods.

One thing should become clear. Whatever the causes, it makes perfect scientific sense to look at a much, much

---

[28] Although there seems to be a drag effect so that warming and cooling appear in cycles after the variations in solar insolation due to the other positive and negative feedbacks in Earth's complex thermostatic system. See the explanation with figure (18-9) in Langmuir and Broecker, 544–555. For the effect of positive and negative feedbacks see Peters, 144–148. If that weren't enough complexity, we find CO_2 ppm levels regularly oscillating over the last 420,000 years in 100,000 cycles, going up to 280 ppm (accompanied by a rise in temperature) and falling to about 200 ppm (accompanied by temperature cooling)—*all prior to any human contribution,* and generally correlated with the Milankovitch cycles. See the chart in Peters, 215, based upon J. R. Petit, "Climate and atmospheric history of the past 420,000 years from the Vostok ice core, Antarctica," *Nature* 399 (June 1999): 429–436.

greater expanse of time in regard to temperature oscillations on Earth, and not just in the last hundred and fifty years, as the global warming folk tend to do. And that forces us to look at a greater range of complex causes over a greater range of time than merely the amount of CO_2 in the atmosphere since the mid-nineteenth century. That broader view is more scientific, rather than less.

If, for example, we hopped way back about 175 million years ago, to the middle of the Jurassic period with all its interesting dinosaurs, we'd experience a much balmier climate than today, with the average temperatures about 6° F warmer (and with about seven times the amount of CO_2 in the atmosphere).

To take another example on a relatively less distant and less vast scale, over the last 1.8 million years, Earth has undergone a kind of temperature oscillation cycle between 100,000 years of bitter cold and glacial advance, followed by 10,000 years of warmth with glacial melting. We are currently at the end of a 10,000 year warm period called the Holocene. Even here, there is variation. For example, the Eemian warm period about 125,000 years ago was warmer than our current warm period, the Holocene, by several degrees.

As noted, according to this oscillation cycle, we're now at the end of the Holocene's 10,000 plus year cycle of warmth, about to enter 100,000 of cold.[29] This is not some Right Wing conjecture to undermine the global warming debate. The simple scientific truth is that the temperature data we've gathered over the last 420,000 years shows periodic, far longer ice ages of 100,000 years, punctuated

---

[29] See the fine and vivid layperson's explanation given by Harvard-educated geologist, E. Kirsten Peters in *The Whole Story of Climate*, 16–22.

by much shorter warmer periods of about 10,000 years. If this data holds, then we're about to come to the end of our happy warmer Holocene period. "Roughly speaking," notes geologist E. Kirsten Peters, "if we expect natural climate rhythms to continue as they have, Earth appears quite ready for a hundred thousand years of deep-freeze cold, with glaciers burying much of the lands many of us inhabit."[30] And what if we add to this the possibility of entering another Maunder Minimum in 2030?

The Big Effect of Little Changes

Whether we are going to be hotter or colder, we must understand the enormous effect that seemingly little bumps in temperature, either way, have on ecosystems—and here, we'll need to include human beings as well.

The whole point of the Left is that human activity can easily knock things off balance, and that seemingly little knock can have astoundingly destructive consequences. Let's use the example of the mountain pine bark beetle to illustrate.[31]

The mountain pine bark beetle is not an invasive species; it's actually native to our North American western pine forests. Our western forests are now splotched with

---

[30] Peters, 140–141.

[31] For overviews, see http://ngm.nationalgeographic.com/2015/04/pine-beetles/rosner-text; "Mountain Pine Beetle," *National Park Service*, https://www.nps.gov/romo/learn/nature/mtn_pine_beetle_background.htm; and "Mountain Pine Beetle Epidemic," *U.S. Forest Service*, https://www.fs.usda.gov/detail/mbr/home/?cid=stelprdb5139168. For an extensive list of scientific research on the mountain pine beetle epidemic see the website of the Western Bark Beetle Research Group at http://www.usu.edu/beetle/pubs_2010.htm.

great patches of dead trees, millions and millions of acres of them, courtesy of this little, seemingly innocuous insect. They have been killers of trees previously, but only moderately, here and there, not enough to get noticed. The carnage they caused was quite minimal, kept naturally within the limits of the forest ecology. But now they are an official epidemic, creating acres upon acres upon acres of dead forests, which not only ruins the complex ecology of the infested area but also sets up millions of acres of kindling just waiting to flare up into epic forest fires.

What caused the epidemic? Two things: one of them certainly human-made, and one of them potentially so. First, we human beings don't like forest fires, and as Smoky the Bear warned us for years, we need to do everything we can to prevent them. The truth, however, is that good intentions don't always yield good results. While not paving the road to hell in this instance, our stopping natural burning of forests results in greater and greater piles of dead trees and limbs which make any fire that does manage to break out into a mega-inferno. Moreover, all that downed and rotting wood that hasn't been periodically burned creates a better and better habitat for beetle reproduction, and more beetles means even more dead trees on the great kindling piles waiting to flare up.

Second, and even more interesting, for whatever reason there happens to have been much warmer and much drier conditions for about the last decade or so over the region where the mountain pine bark beetle resides. An extended warm season means a much longer time for the beetle to do its damage; even more ominous, it adds extra breeding seasons. Whether or not this warmer spell is the result of human CO_2 emissions, it does show us quite clearly that a little bump in temperature can have drastic environmental consequences.

The upshot is this: The Right may respond to the Left's worry about a few degrees temperature rise with a smirky, "Well, I'd like it to be a few degrees warmer!" attitude, but this shows culpable ignorance of the devastating effects that a rise of a few degrees *has already made.* The mountain pine bark beetle epidemic doesn't prove that the warming is caused by us, but it does demonstrate very clearly how destructive so small a rise could be.

We may look to our own species for another example. The Romans prospered in part because they had really good weather during a period of general climate warmth called, eponymously, the Roman Warm Period (c. 250 BC–AD 400). Why did the Roman Empire fall, and the West enter the Dark Ages? In part, because Europe went from longer, dryer summers, to significantly colder and wetter summers, and crops failed year after year.

But then Europe became warmer during the so-called Medieval Warming Period (c. AD 950–1300). As a result, civilization recovered and crops of all kind blossomed over higher latitudes. Then, in the darkest of centuries, the century of the Black Plague, Europe's climate swung back to a long, cold spell, where cold and wet summers destroyed crops and caused famine—the so-called Mini Ice Age, which didn't let up unto the mid-1800s.[32]

As we've noted in a previous section in this chapter, since about 1850 we've enjoyed another warm period in the cycle, and so crops have increased and civilization has

[32] See Brian Fagen, *The Great Warming: Climate Change and the Rise and Fall of Civilizations* (New York: Bloomsbury Press, 2006); and *The Little Ice Age: How Climate Made History, 1300–1850* (New York: Basic Books, 2000).

flourished, an effect seemingly magnified by the technological and chemical agricultural enhancements that mark the Industrial Revolution, the very ones that produce more CO_2.

What will happen next in our climate cycle and what effects will it have on our civilizations? Again, that is a matter of debate. But we can draw one important conclusion: while Earth itself is robust, considered as a biosphere, human civilization is deeply susceptible, in its flourishing or crumbling, to small changes in climate.

And if human civilizations are that susceptible, then other creatures in their ecosystems are susceptible as well. Slight variations can have major effects on all living things. We know this occurs because of natural variations; therefore, it would seem obvious that human-made variations could have significant effects as well.

And So . . . ?

What can we draw from all of this? *To begin with* the material we just covered, we know that climate swings in Earth's history are normal, and in fact, fairly predictable over longer periods—all before human beings started adding lots of extra CO_2 into the atmosphere. The Right has generally been the one to point to these extra factors, and these factors must be part of the debate.

Second, pointing this out does not, as such, settle the global warming debate. Our thermostatic system is wonderfully effective, but also dauntingly complex, so complex that we do not yet fully understand it. It might be, as the Left maintains, that drastically increasing CO_2 emissions by human beings during the last hundred and fifty years could be just what it takes to throw Earth's thermostat off kilter. Or, it may be that we're entering a naturally far cooler period, and global warming might make it more bearable.

Third, while we may have trouble sorting out all the factors that effect and affect climate variation over time, there is no doubt that our climate does vary naturally, and even more interesting, very slight variations can cause major good and bad effects on even more delicate ecosystems, especially the most delicate and complex of all, human civilizations. We know this because it happened even before the Industrial Revolution.

Fourth, because of this, we must be careful going forward. We can't run roughshod over nature and expect that we will avoid negative results. Human beings can do stupid, short-sighted, and self-destructive things that serve their pleasures, their passions, and their goals, and in doing so disregard the wonderful order of nature that sustains them.

Think how short a space of Earth-time our Industrial Age actually takes up: about .00000375 percent of our four-plus billion years. It seems an act of hubris to think that we can understand the full effects of something so significant as the Industrial Revolution, given the small amount of time we've been running this experiment.

But that brings us to a *fifth* point. The very same point must be made about such "experiments" as the Sexual Revolution. If the Left is willing to admit that drastic, unprecedented human-made changes in short periods of time can have unpredicted, even more drastic ill effects in regard to CO_2 production brought about by the Industrial Revolution, then it ought to take a much more serious and sobering look at the possibility that drastic, unprecedented human-made changes in sexuality in historically short periods of time can have unpredicted, even more drastic ill effects on human nature and human society.

Sixth and last, there is a very interesting aspect of the debate about global warming. The argument for global warming is based upon the general recognition—which has become more and more deeply understood through the last half-century of scientific discoveries—that the origin and development of the universe is finely tuned, precisely orchestrated from its very beginning and throughout its development over billions of years, right down to the Earth's extraordinarily delicately balanced biosphere that allows for the existence and flourishing of complex life. The global warming argument is focused on a slice of that delicately balanced biosphere, our atmosphere.

As I said, many—I include myself—believe that these layers and layers of just-rightness that make our life possible on Earth point to a theistic conclusion: it isn't all just a cosmic accident; it's too well orchestrated, too amazingly complex and intricate, for it to have been a matter of chance. It points to a divine cause.

To put it in Catholic (big "C") terms from the Catechism: "Created in God's image and called to know and love him, the person who seeks God discovers certain ways of coming to know him. These are also called proofs for the existence of God, not in the sense of proofs in the natural sciences"—that is, one cannot perform a God experiment, proving His existence, in the same way one can perform an experiment to prove the existence of oxygen—"but rather in the sense of 'converging and convincing arguments,' which allow us to attain certainty about the truth" (31).

It certainly seems that the more we look into the layers upon layers of intricate ordered complexity that allow for the existence of life on Earth, the more we find "converging and convincing arguments" for the existence of God.

Papal Coda on catholic/Catholic Ecology

Since we began this long chapter with Pope Francis' encyclical *Laudato si'*, it would be fitting to end with it as well. Pope Francis did come down on the side of the Left in regard to global warming, but he also made clear that the whole question of global warming is part of a larger set of concerns which include moral ecology as well.

> A sense of deep communion with the rest of nature cannot be real if our hearts lack tenderness, compassion and concern for our fellow human beings. It is clearly inconsistent to combat trafficking in endangered species while remaining completely indifferent to human trafficking, unconcerned about the poor, or undertaking to destroy another human being deemed unwanted. . . . Everything is connected. Concern for the environment thus needs to be joined to a sincere love for our fellow human beings and an unwavering commitment to resolving the problems of society.[33]

Quoting St. John Paul II's *Centesimus Annus*, Pope Francis reaffirms this connection. "Not only has God given the earth to man, who must use it with respect for the original good purpose for which it was given, but, man too

---

[33] *Laudato si'*, §91.

is God's gift to man. He must therefore respect the natural and moral structure with which he has been endowed."[34] "Since everything is interrelated," Pope Francis continues, "concern for the protection of nature is also incompatible with the justification of abortion."[35]

And that brings us back from our consideration of global warming to our larger consideration of the relationship of natural ecology and moral ecology.

---

[34] Ibid., §115.
[35] Ibid., §120.

CHAPTER SEVEN

The Great Pyramid of Beings, Natural Law, the Ecological Hierarchy, and Your Own Ecosystem

The Right Kind of Anthropism

Near the end of the last chapter, I noted that many have understood the amazing fine-tuning of nature to imply a kind of argument for the existence of God, drawing out inferences from the fact that our life here on Earth is dependent on a long series of intricately interconnected and delicate conditions, from the Big Bang all the way down to our wonderfully temperate, life-giving biosphere. A little bit of fine-tuning here and there and we might not be tempted to draw theistic conclusions. But layer upon layer from the very beginning right down to the present day seems to point to the existence of an Intelligent Cause, a Wise Creator.

There is actually a name for this type of argument, the argument from what's called the Anthropic Cosmological Principle. In contrast to what Pope Francis called "tyrannical anthropocentricism,"[1] wherein human beings attempt to ruthlessly master nature, this kind of anthropic account simply describes our place in the universe and what it took

---

[1]   See *Laudato si'*, §68.

to get us here. It is a recognition that the conditions that have allowed for the development and sustenance of life, and ultimately human life (*anthrōpos* is Greek for human being), are astoundingly complex, delicate, and precise. It is called "anthropic" because we human beings are at the developmental peak of the great multitude of beings on Earth, the first and only being we know of that is capable of science.

This is a statement of both horizontal and vertical fact. When we look horizontally in time at the millions upon millions of years of evolutionary development of complex life, we rational animals are very late arrivals, arising only with the last 70,000 to 10,000 years, depending on how one assesses things. (We are not speaking about some remote "ancestor" walking upright, but the expression of qualitatively significant intelligence, such as in the cave paintings at Lascaux, the verifiable use of language, or the agricultural revolution.)

When we look vertically at the beings now inhabiting Earth, we are at the pinnacle of animal capabilities, again the result not of strength or speed, but of our rational capacities. (To repeat, we are speaking about qualitatively different expressions of intelligence, such as the development of Euclidean Geometry or Calculus, as compared to the rudimentary counting capacities of, say, crows.)

So, when we look at the fantastic unfolding of the cosmos, we contain within us the highest peak of the potentialities of the chemical elements first birthed in the Big Bang, not only in how they are the material that makes possible our natural capacity to think and act (constituting our living bodies, senses, and brains), but in our singular, scientific achievement of discovering the chemical elements and their order as represented in the Periodic Table.

The same is true for physics and biology. All beings obey the laws of physics, and these laws provide the framework for the physical reality that makes life possible, but we're the only beings who've discovered these laws. Biologically, there is a countless multitude of interesting living creatures on Earth, but we're the only ones whose biology includes the capacity for the science of biology.

That's the original meaning of the *Anthropic* Cosmological Principle: the conditions of the universe have to have been of the kind necessary for human beings to have developed sufficiently to have advanced science—because that *is* what we are in fact doing.[2]

A lot of things had to be just right in order for human beings to develop to the condition where they could discover that a lot of things had to be just right in order for human beings to discover that a lot of things had to be just right for them to discover things as scientists. Think about that—and add the fact that I've stated only a small fraction of the evidence.[3]

---

[2] I'm slightly paraphrasing Brandon Carter's formulation, as he is the person credited with naming the "anthropic principle." In his words, "What we can expect to observe," as scientists, "must be restricted by the conditions necessary for our presence as observers." Since human beings obviously are here, they are intelligent, and their intelligence has developed to a point where they are capable of advanced science. Whatever precise conditions make all that possible, we know that these conditions did and do in fact exist, otherwise we wouldn't be here. See Brandon Carter, "Large Number Coincidences and the Anthropic Principle in Cosmology," in M. S. Longair, ed., *Confrontation of Cosmological Theories with Observational Data* (Dordrecht, NL: Reidel, 1974), 291–298.

[3] For a much fuller account, see Guillermo Gonzalez and Jay Richards, *The Privileged Planet: How Our Place in the Cosmos Is Designed for Discovery* (Washington, DC: Regnery Publishing, 2004); and my and Jonathan Witt's *A Meaningful World: How the Arts and Sciences Reveal the Genius of Nature* (Downers Grove, IL: InterVarsity Press, 2006).

The Theological View at the Top of the Pyramid

Now I'm going to (somewhat) restate the Anthropic Cosmological Principle *theologically*, straight from the *Catechism of the Catholic Church*—one of my favorite sections—which puts human beings on the top of the pyramid of life.

> Man, though made of body and soul, is a unity. Through his very bodily condition he sums up in himself the elements of the material world. Through him they are thus brought to their highest perfection and can raise their voice in praise freely given to the Creator. For this reason man may not despise his bodily life. Rather he is obliged to regard his body as good and to hold it in honor since God has created it and will raise it up on the last day. (364)

We are indeed made up, bodily, of the chemical elements, some of which were fused together at the very origins of the universe; others were cooked up in stars over billions of years. While the human body contains, naturally, about twenty-five of the hundred-plus chemical elements, 99 percent of it is made up of only six elements: oxygen (65 percent), carbon (18.5 percent), hydrogen (9.5 percent), nitrogen (3.2 percent), calcium (1.5 percent), and phosphorus (1.0 percent).

Of course, the elements aren't just dumped into a body shell like so many cake ingredients, but embedded in complex chemical compounds, such as lipids (carbon and hydrogen), proteins made up of amino acids (carbon, hydrogen, oxygen, nitrogen), DNA made up of nucleic acids (hydrogen, carbon, oxygen, nitrogen, phosphorus), and so on. The elements making up compounds are in turn part of more complex structures (such as cells and their parts) and processes (such as enzymes acting as catalysts to speed up needed chemical reactions in the body). These are parts of a startlingly complex orchestration of organs, each with its own function, all of which work in magnificent unity in all sorts of living creatures, so that they can fly, swim, run, sleep, see, hear, smell, taste, flit through tree branches, crawl over rocks, scamper in savannahs, hunt in darkness, hunt in daytime, mate in season, chew, sting, bite, claw, howl, coo, and cackle.

If we pause at this level of the pyramid, it is clear that we have a great deal in common with the other animals inhabiting Earth: bones, lungs, intestines, hearts, blood, limbs, eyes, noses, ears, tongues, skin sensitive to touch, brains—all pretty much standard equipment with variations among the species. Animals mate; so do we. Animals eat; so do we. Animals feel fear; so do we. Animals express something like anger and joy and sadness. Animals are able to judge different possibilities for action, and some even educate their young in hunting and other aspects of their particular mode of life.

But in one living creature, human beings, these same chemical elements, woven into the intricate and integrated hierarchical anatomical order of the human body, make possible the peculiar activities of human rationality, which includes both engaging in science (with dizzyingly complex mathematics, microscopes, telescopes, binoculars, computers, beakers, Bunsen burners, and thermometers), and raising an articulate voice in praise freely given to the Creator in speech and song (that is, in philosophical, theological, and scientific affirmation of the beauty and wisdom of the orders of nature and in

complex vocal harmony celebrating the glories of creation and redemption, accompanied by pipe organs, pianos,
violins, violas, trumpets, kettle drums, flutes, oboes, clari-
nets, and French horns).

Please reread that passage from the Catechism slowly.
You might have missed what was really being said here, so
I'll add italics for emphasis: "Man, though made of body and
soul, is a unity. Through his very bodily condition he sums
up in himself the *elements* of the material world. Through
him *they* are thus brought to *their highest perfection* and can
raise *their voice* in praise freely given to the Creator."

We have to shake ourselves and wake ourselves gram-
matically here, because we, in our stumbling attempts to
deal with pronouns often use a plural pronoun (e.g., "they"
or "them") for singular subjects (like "he" or "she," "Bob"
or "Jane"). But the editors of the Catechism are unbend-
ing grammarians. Thus "they," "their highest perfection,"
and "their voice" all refer to the chemical elements. The
Church really is saying—with the affirmation of science—
that carbon, hydrogen, oxygen, nitrogen, and so on, find
their highest perfection in songs of praise to the Creator.
Handel's *Messiah* is, we might say, the ultimate manifestation of their respective chemical potentialities, as these
chemical elements exist in the bodily structure of the
only creature that can make these elements (as part of
chemical compounds, which are part of cells, which are
part of organs like the tongue, teeth, vocal cords, and the
human brain) give praise to God. It isn't just the chemical
elements that are brought to this perfection, but all our
animal capacities as well.

But these same elements, born in the Big Bang and
nurtured in the furnaces of countless stars, likewise find
their perfection as chemical elements in the chemical

compounds, making up the cells, making up the organs such as the human eye, the hand, and the brain, which scientists use to know the vast and intricate complexities of nature, including human nature. That too is a mode of praise for the Creator of these elements that could have such magnificent potentialities.

On the Catholic understanding, this all fits together because the existence of God can be known with certainty by our natural rationality through an investigation of nature: the Orderer can be known through the order, the Cause through the effects.[4] And that too is cause for praise.

The Natural Law

The pyramid I've just described has another name: the natural law—not the law or laws of nature, but the natural law: the law of human nature. This is obviously a different understanding of law than we are familiar with, so a bit of explaining is in order.

The natural law account of human nature actually goes back to ancient Greek philosophy, primarily to Aristotle and later to the Roman Stoics, but Christians of the first centuries believed it to be an accurate account of human nature, especially human moral nature, and so adopted it (with some modifications). St. Thomas Aquinas famously provides the most succinct statement of it in his *Summa Theologiae*.[5]

---

[4] *Catechism of the Catholic Church*, 31–38.

[5] St. Thomas Aquinas, *Summa Theologiae,* I-II, q. 94, a. 2. St. Thomas begins by noting that "the first principle of practical reason is one founded on the notion of good, viz. that 'good is that which all things seek after.' Hence this is the first precept of law, that 'good is to be done and pursued, and evil is to be avoided.' All other precepts of the natural law are based

The natural law is built upon a larger account of nature, an account that reasons in the following common sense

upon this: so that whatever the practical reason naturally apprehends as man's good (or evil) belongs to the precepts of the natural law as something to be done or avoided." To make it perfectly clear what St. Thomas is saying, we need to understand that in order to reason well about what is good for us, we must have actual knowledge of what a human being really is. He continues, "Since, however, good has the nature of an end, and evil, the nature of a contrary, hence it is that all those things to which man has a natural inclination, are naturally apprehended by reason as being good, and consequently as objects of pursuit, and their contraries as evil, and objects of avoidance." Again, to avoid confusions, St. Thomas asserts that each kind of creature has built-in inclinations that drive it toward what is actually good for it, so, trout *want* to swim and mate according to the ways of a trout. Likewise, human beings have built-in inclinations, but unlike the trout, they have no instinct that guides these inclinations toward their proper goal of human perfection; instead, we must use reason and free moral choice. In the following, then, Thomas is not saying that we should follow any inclination we may happen to have, but that we have inclinations which, if properly ordered by reason and virtue, will bring us to do what is actually good for us. We have a hierarchy of inclinations that define the fullness of our nature, and hence what is morally good for us to choose. In his words,

Wherefore according to the order of natural inclinations, is the order of the precepts of the natural law. Because in man there is first of all an inclination to good in accordance with the nature which he has in common with all substances: inasmuch as every substance seeks the preservation of its own being, according to its nature: and by reason of this inclination, whatever is a means of preserving human life, and of warding off its obstacles, belongs to the natural law. Secondly, there is in man an inclination to things that pertain to him more specially, according to that nature which he has in common with other animals: and in virtue of this inclination, those things are said to belong to the natural law, 'which nature has taught to all animals' such as sexual intercourse, education of offspring and so forth. Thirdly, there is in man an inclination to good, according to the nature of his reason, which nature is proper to him: thus man has a natural inclination to know the truth about God, and to live in society: and in this respect, whatever pertains to this inclination belongs to the natural law; for instance, to shun ignorance, to avoid offending those among whom one has to live, and other such things regarding the above inclination.

way. Each particular kind of being—a crow, a salamander, a turtle, a hawk, a trout—has its own defined good: what perfects that kind of being, makes it healthy and flourishing rather than sickly or just plain dead. Each kind of being therefore has its own particular kind of "law," that is, a set of specific abilities that define the characteristic activities that are good for it, and as a consequence, a set that are bad for it *as that particular kind of creature*. So, to be somewhat whimsical, we may speak of "turtle law" or "crow law" or "hawk law." All that we mean by "law" here is that each kind of living creature has its own set of things that are good for it, being what it is, and consequently, bad for it, being what it is. To follow its law means to pursue what is good for its own particular specific nature.

Let's look at trout law. A trout is built to live in freshwater streams. Pulling it out of the water will kill it; living things need oxygen, but a trout is built to obtain oxygen from the water through its gills. A freshwater trout is a hyperosmotic fish, made to absorb water to offset the natural osmotic tendency of the solutes (dissolved substances) in its body to move from higher to lower concentrations, that is, from the higher concentration of solutes inside its cells to the water outside where the solute concentration is lower. Putting the trout into the ocean will kill it because the solute content of the salt water is greater than the solute content in the freshwater trout's cells, so water will be drawn osmotically out of the trout's system, literally drying it up.

But there are other kinds of violations of trout law. Agricultural runoff in freshwater streams, which includes nasty bacteria, pesticides, herbicides, hormones, and fertilizers, also kills or significantly harms freshwater trout. Trout law is also violated by increases in water temperature, such as caused by nuclear power plants or coal-burning plants pouring heated water into lakes and streams, because trout are built to function within a particular slim temperature range. Hence, slight increases in temperature kill trout in streams. Or, to finish with an interesting twist, as it turns out, the Pill violates trout law. Women who take the Pill "secrete" (urinate), as they are wont to do by nature, but the synthetic estrogen finds its way into the water supply via sewage treatment plants, and renders fish in the wild unable to reproduce, as researcher Karen Kidd and her colleagues document in their study, "Collapse of a fish population after exposure to a synthetic estrogen."[6]

Now one might think, following this account of trout law, that the law of human being would be called human being law, but, as it turns out historically, the law of human being was designated the natural law. As with the trout law, the natural law examines human being in all its complexity and asks the question, "What is good for human beings *as* human beings?" What makes us what we are, as a particular species, and hence defines what is good for us?

The important difference in regard to human beings is that, unlike other animals, we are not guided by instinct to do the things that are good for our nature. As noted above in our chapter on obesity, other animals naturally eat the kinds of food that are good for them as defined by

---

[6] Karen A. Kidd, et al., "Collapse of a fish population after exposure to a synthetic estrogen," *Proceedings of the National Academy of Sciences of the United States of America* 104, no. 2 (May 2007): 8897–8901; and the popular report on this, John Roach, "Sex-Changing Chemicals Can Wipe Out Fish," *National Geographic News*, May 21, 2007, http://news.national-geographic.com/news/2007/05/070521-sex-fish.html.

the particular kinds of animals that they are. We human beings have to figure out what to eat, using our reason, but can also use our reason and freely choose to produce and eat things that are harmful. The same is true for sexuality. Other animals are governed by seasons of heat in regard to the kind of mating appropriate for their species. We human beings have animal sexual desire but no guiding instinct that governs our mating; therefore, we are free to use our reason to come up with the most elaborately harmful sexual practices, as noted in lurid and horrid detail in the chapter on pornography. So, unlike other animals, human beings need moral virtue, in this case two different kinds of temperance, to avoid the self-destructive vices of gluttony and lust.

Note, in the natural law, that moral commands are not issued to us externally. They arise from our nature and help us to live according to our nature, but they are not instinctual. We must use our reason to discern our nature and then choose the good of our nature, aided by good habits, that is, the virtues.

The highest part of our nature, according to the natural law, is our capacity to know the truth—that is, to use our reason for what it is made to do—and we are the only animals that can do it. We are built to know the truth about nature, about ourselves, and about God. But the natural law adds that it is also part of our highest capacity to live in community in rational friendship. To put it in its old-fashioned but wonderfully accurate form, we are by nature rational, political animals (political here meaning something roughly equivalent to our word "social"). False-hood goes against our nature, but so does loneliness: both violate the natural law, the law of human nature.

To draw all of this together, we can see that both

trout and human beings must have the right *environment* that allows them to flourish as the kind of creatures that they are by nature. They have different Laws, but their respective Laws have significant commonalities. Both need clean water because water is essential to both of their respective biologies. Both need good food, unpoisoned by chemicals that harm their growth, metabolism, digestion, and respiration. Both have to reproduce. Each is harmed by the lack of what it needs according to its nature, or by violations of its nature from outside.

But there is a great difference: human beings are the only ones that can harm both themselves and a significant number of other creatures, either directly or by some kind of pollution, environmental or moral. And that is, again, because of the capacities of reason and free moral choice that put human beings on the top of the pyramid of beings.

So, to repeat, we are on top of the pyramid for two related reasons: first, we have the most extensive natural capacities of anything below us, whether living (animal or plant) or nonliving (chemical elements and compounds, etc.), and second, because we are literally constituted by a representative range of all the things below us, from chemical compounds, cells, metabolic systems, the various basic animal organs and functions, all of which allow us to carry on our particular, unique capacities for reason and moral choice.

Now that we've gotten a general outline of the pyramid of beings and its representation in the natural law, we need to understand how this might fit into a standard ecology textbook account of the ecological hierarchy.

The Ecological Hierarchy

Let's get the textbook account down before we go on to see how it fits with what we've covered above. Ecologists use somewhat different terms to describe the interconnected and interdependent *levels* of the nonliving and living hierarchy of conditions and diversity of beings that make up our ecological hierarchical system, but we can settle on some common aspects.[7]

The largest and most comprehensive level, from the perspective of ecologists, is the *biosphere* (or *ecosphere*, as some call it) which includes all the living and nonliving beings and conditions that define the complexity of our life on Earth. Our biosphere includes the amount of liquid water and its distribution, wind and water currents that make life possible, down through all the kinds of living creatures that populate the globe, from plankton and bacteria to elephants and human beings.

The *biosphere* is the Big Picture level, if one takes that picture from the perspective of outside Earth, viewing Earth as a great, round, self-contained terrarium floating in space, a sphere enclosing within its atmosphere all that is needed to generate and sustain the nearly uncountable diversity of life we enjoy. All that is needed from outside our floating terrarium, so ecologists say, is the input of energy from the Sun through the earth's atmosphere. The

---

[7] For the following analysis I am relying on a number of college-level textbooks which sum up the best and latest in the science of ecology. Eugene Odum and Gary Barrett, *Fundamentals of Ecology*, 5th ed. (Belmont, CA: Thomson Brooks/Cole, 2005); David Krohne, *General Ecology*, 2nd ed. (Belmont, CA: Thomson Brooks/Cole, 2001); and Robert Ricklefs and Rich Relyea, *Ecology: the Economy of Nature* (New York: W. H. Freeman and Company, 2014).

input of solar energy is transformed by plants through photosynthesis into the biological foundation of all other living things, providing oxygen for their respiration and food for the food chain, from herbivores to carnivores. Without this food base, there could be no greater forms of life.

Since energy cannot be created or destroyed, as the first law of thermodynamics states, the living sphere of Earth exhales its expended energy in the form of heat through its atmosphere back out into space. In the continual transformation of that energy from light to heat, ingesting and exhaling, the great terrarium Earth continually develops and diversifies life within.

As we're well aware, life within the biosphere isn't an undifferentiated and disordered mass. Living things within our terrarium Earth develop and diversify in layers of interdependent, hierarchical, ecological order. In that order, there are obviously *individual organisms* at different times and places—a catfish, a skunk, a red oak, a nematode, a crawdad—that ecologists study.

But these individual organisms do not arise singly, in abstraction from place and time. They are members of *species* living in actual *populations* in particular areas at particular times.

Yet, just as obvious, single populations don't exist in isolation. In any particular area and time, we find more than one kind of creature; in fact, there are many populations of different species coexisting in the same place and time, and doing so interdependently in what ecologists have named a *community*.

This community of diverse creatures living together under one part of Earth's roof isn't just floating in abstraction. It depends upon and interacts with the nonliving and physical elements, such as the water, soil, air, and climate of the area where they all happen to live. So taking all the living and nonliving elements together in a particular time and place, we have an *ecosystem*, the next level in the ecological hierarchy, and the one that provides the clearest, definitive understanding of what ecology as a science studies.

The reason is that the *ecosystem* is the first complete level, containing all that's necessary for ongoing sustenance of life in a complex hierarchy: *individual organisms* arise from *populations* of particular *species* that depend on the particular living and nonliving elements of the *community* (sunlight, water, and minerals, plants, and other animals) to live.

The ecosystem level, as containing (generally) all that is necessary for the ongoing sustenance of the diverse creatures that inhabit it, has also been called a natural *economy*, and for good reason. An economy, if we strip away or abstract from the human artificial aspects associated with our own economy, is the ordered system of living beings in community, beings who eat (take in energy), live, and reproduce. The economy of the ecosystem consists of all that is necessary for the healthy survival of a community of living beings in a particular time and place. Plants eat sunshine, water, and minerals from the soil and give off oxygen; mice and rabbits eat plants and their seeds and give back to the plants CO_2, manure, and their decomposed bodies; hawks eat rabbits and mice.

Economy, like the word ecosystem, describes the complex of interdependent relationships that allow for a mutually beneficial, living system in one place to be *sustained* over time. At least to our ears, the word "economy" focuses more on how each member of the human "ecosystem" makes a living, but we need to keep this larger understanding of economy in mind.

We'll come back to the ecosystem level, but let's return to our account of the ecological hierarchy. There are yet more comprehensive levels beyond the ecosystem that some ecologists use, the next largest being a *landscape*, wherein the scientist stands farther back and studies clusters of overlapping ecosystems.

These landscapes aren't homogeneous, but exist in certain kinds of definable regions, in terms of climate, geography, and vegetation, such as tropical rain forests, woodlands, seasonal forests, or tundras. These regions are called *biomes*.

The various *biomes* are what make up the earthly part of the earth's *biosphere*, which is, again, the most comprehensive level of the hierarchy used by ecologists.

Looking at the whole structure, we have what ecologists Eugene Odum and Gary Barrett call a kind of *nested hierarchy*, where "each level is made up of groups of lower-level units,"[8] so that the biosphere is made up of various biomes, each biome is made up of various landscapes, each landscape is made up of various ecosystems, each ecosystem is made up of various populations of species, and each population is made up of particular individual organisms. (And, if we continue downward, or inward, each organism is made up of organ systems, each of which is made up of particular tissues, each of which is made up of particular cells, each of which is made up of particular chemical compounds, and each of which is made up of particular chemical elements.)

---

[8] Odum and Barrett, 7.

Discover Your Own Ecosystem

These very general, abstract technical terms, we mustn't forget, don't actually themselves exist like some kind of rarified Platonic form. There is no such thing, for example, as a generic ecosystem. They are all quite particular, and for the sake of not living a life abstracted from nature, we really ought to be much more aware of the particular ecosystem in which we live, so that we can actually experience, deeply, the astounding diversity of living and nonliving things that make up its dynamic yet stable harmony.

So as not to fall into the folly of giving advice and not taking it myself, my children and I took an inventory of ours. We now live in something like the suburbs, one that borders in the back on a field, with several acres of woods beyond that (the field and woods belonging to someone else). There is a stream, a very small one, at the bottom of the gulley in the woods. That's our particular ecosystem (or at least a piece of it). What did we find in it?

Of course, there is sunshine and rain, fueling the growth of a significant diversity of plants, both flowering and non-flowering. The grasses in the field are too hard to identify (at least without a better guide than we've got), but flowering plants are less so. We found common buttercup, lesser snapdragon, both hairy and blue-stemmed goldenrod, Barnaby's thistle, king devil, both common and red-seeded dandelion, smooth and round-leaved yellow violet, blue phlox, plantain, pokeweed (the inviting berries of which, my youngest daughter insists I report, are poisonous to mammals, but not to songbirds), common milkweed, stinging nettle (which I could do without), multiflora rose (the most pernicious of invasive plants I've encountered), Indian strawberry (sometimes called mock strawberry), both white and alsike clover, jewelweed, wild carrot (or Queen Anne's Lace, if you prefer), and (happily) wild blackberry.

These all provide energy for a great number of insects and animals. On a single survey, we found ladybugs, stink bugs, leaf hoppers, plant hoppers, katydids, crickets, grass-hoppers, lacewings, and, feeding on them, assassin bugs, jumping spiders, crab spiders, and funnel spiders.

On the next level of the eating hierarchy, we've got quite a few mud dauber wasps, who consume the spiders. (We had organ pipe mud daubers build a nest on the back of the old couch awaiting disposal in our garage.) Of course we've got bumble bees and yellow jackets, but not enough of the former and too many of the latter (al-though the adult yellow jackets do glean pestiferous insects to feed to their larvae). We have a few dragonflies, which spend their long nymph stage down in the stream gobbling mosquito larvae and tadpoles, and then after a fantastic metamorphosis come up to the field to mate and dine on adult mosquitos, moths, butterflies, and even smaller dragonflies.

A more careful look at the grass in the field yields the characteristic bubbly white spit glommed onto a stem. Hiding within the froth there's a spit bug, which is really the nymph of the adult froghopper. The latter name comes, one assumes, from the froghopper's amazing jumping ability, up to thirty inches straight up in the air—which, on rough calculation, would be something like my being able to jump to the top of a forty-story building from the ground.

And there's our favorite of all, the monarch butter-fly who lays eggs on the milkweed so that (to our way of looking at things) we can take the yellow, black, and white-striped caterpillars into our house, whilst they systematically crunch away at the milkweed leaves, so we can witness, once again, their magnificent metamorphosis from the comfort of our kitchen table. (Just this morning, we had one assume its position, dangling upside down in an inverted question mark, becoming a chrysalis tied up with a golden thread around the top.)

We've also got a fair number of cabbage whites and clouded sulphur butterflies flitting about the field. As with many others, I am far less enamored by the caterpillars of gypsy moths devouring the leaves of the trees and am thankful for the counterattack provided by the wasps, ants, spiders, shrews, raccoons, blue jays, and starlings that eat them at the various stages of their life cycle.

Speaking of trees, in the woods we've got—or technically, our neighbors have—red maple, sugar maple, white oak, red oak, shagbark hickory, dogwood, quaking aspen, black cherry, mulberry, staghorn sumac, yellow birch, ash, and a few pines scattered throughout.

On the floor of the woods, quietly consuming the dead leaves, branches, and other organic detritus, are our bottom feeders: mushrooms. I will confess that it was not until writing this book that I paid any but the most minimal attention to the varieties of wild mushrooms, but on a fairly quick, hour-long walking survey in the woods I found a two-colored bolete, bitter bolete, false and true puffball, chanterelle, club-footed clitocybe, scarlet elfcup, and my personal favorite, both for its vibrant color and even more vibrant name, the vomiting russula, which tells you what happens if you eat one raw.

Our modest ecosystem includes a goodly number of birds. At this time of year, we've got sparrows, goldfinch, robins, bluebirds, crows, doves, red-tailed hawks, turkey vultures and wild turkeys, blue jays, cardinals, starlings, purple finches, swallows, mockingbirds, meadowlarks, and, for some reason, a whole lot of killdeer. Happily, they keep the insect population down (with the hawks keeping the mice, shrews, and rabbits under control).

We've got a lot of rabbits this year (eastern cottontail), and for much the same reason, we suspect, too many skunks (one of which sprayed our dog this summer, who promptly bolted into the house to rub off his offended face all over our carpet). We've got field mice, shrews, and moles eating seeds, plants, worms, and grubs, and omnivorous raccoons eating all of them in turn. Frequently, white-tailed deer wander out of the woods at night to forage in the field, and occasionally, we hear a pack of coyotes quite near the house.

We've also recently caught up with an eastern box turtle along the path in the woods, perhaps on her way to eat some blackberries, or some grubs, slugs, worms or other creepy-crawly whatnots inhabiting the floor of the woods. There are also dusky salamanders down in the crick (the diminutive of creek), as well as leopard frogs, crayfish, and eastern newts. An eastern ring-necked snake found its way into our garage a few weeks ago, and a fair number of toads can be found even around our house, especially at dusk.

There we've got it, or rather, a good first go at the diversity of the small ecosystem surrounding our house. If you do your own inventory—which you should—you'll experience firsthand (rather than through a book) what a real ecosystem is, where each piece fits happily into the whole, making up a superbly balanced dynamic yet stable ecological harmony.

You really can't understand what ecology means until you discover in detail the ecosystem of your own home, the ecosystem you pass by every day without much thought. So, again, I commend this exercise to you, the reader, especially if you are grumpily disinclined to do anything in nature beyond mowing some of it and spend most of your time staring at a screen instead of the wonders of nature. That's how you begin to discover your place in the ecological hierarchy in the great pyramid of beings.

We Forgot Something—Ourselves

But have we really found our place if we have forgotten to count ourselves in our ecological survey? If *we* disappeared tomorrow, the woods and the field, the stream with its crayfish, the deer, raccoons, skunks, rabbits, mice, shrews, wild turkeys, all the insects and birds, turtles, snakes, and toads would get along fine. They naturally live, sustainably, in this particular ecosystem. Unlike us, they provide for themselves quite well in this ecosystem because their eating, living, and breeding all occur within the natural limits of this particular area, all the living and nonliving things balancing each other out in equilibrium. For the same reason, all of these living things—minus human beings—don't cause any harmful degradation of the ecosystem upon which they depend for their existence. They don't pollute because they can't. They have a healthy, balanced economy—if we can again use that rough synonym for ecosystem.

But when we include ourselves in our survey, we realize some startling but obvious facts. We are not like the other creatures. We don't live in nests or dens, but have houses built of a multitude of natural and artificial materials, almost all of which were produced elsewhere.

Most of us don't consume food from our own eco-systems, but have it shipped to our stores from multiple different ecosystems in radically different landscapes and biomes (coffee, tea, bananas, oranges, apples). And we have cars to go outside our ecosystems to others nearby, where the grocery stores reside.

All of these types of food—far more varied than any other animals or insect is able to conjure up—take massive amounts of fossil fuels to produce and deliver, from fertilizer and pesticides to gasoline and oil for the farm machinery and trucks.

Unless we have our own well, our water is pumped in from outside of our immediate ecosystem, and we also have these strange wires attached to our house where concentrated energy, produced from coal, gas, or nuclear power, runs everything from our lights to our toaster and computers.

We also have—unlike the spiders, wasps, killdeer, rac-coons, etc.—strange things called books, manufactured from trees in other ecosystems and the thoughts of human beings from other times and places, and these are one of the most definitive signs of our particular nature as human beings. And we now have electronic access to the rest of the world through our computers and smartphones.

Finally, we must admit that the garbage truck arrives promptly every week in our ecosphere to haul off our trash to some other ecosphere (for us, most likely the one near where we used to live some ten miles away).

Could we live, sustainably, entirely within our own ecosystem, as other animals do?

Imagine for a moment what it would be like to try to

survive *where you actually live*, entirely from within your ecosystem, so that you provide all the necessities of water, food, clothing, and shelter from the immediate surrounding area of, say, three or four acres. If you're inclined to bracing and hence clarifying scenarios to energize your imagination, pretend that there has been a sudden, complete interruption of coal and petroleum resources, so that there are no shipments of food into grocery stores, stores which you can't get to anyway because there is no gas for your car. Moreover, water ceases to run from your faucets, because the water plants have no energy to function, and no electricity awaits your various plugs. No trucks come to pick up your trash.

How long would you and your family be able to sustain yourselves?

Caught between the City of Sows or the Feverish City?

Perhaps the reader is expecting me, at this point, to say something like, "And that's why we all need to get back to living *entirely* within our own, local ecosystems, eating only what it takes to survive, and surviving only on what we can find in our immediate environment. In short, we need to live exactly like the animals and plants within each of our own particular ecosystems."

That is a temptation, an age-old one that periodically arises when human beings feel threatened or overburdened or just plain sick or bored of whatever advanced civilization they happen to be living in. It's the temptation of many of today's hardcore back-to-nature environmentalists of the Left, who are really the great, great intellectual grandchildren of the eighteenth-century philosopher Jean-Jacques Rousseau whose two seminal essays, the First and Second Discourses—or more exactly, *Discourse on the Sciences and the Arts* and *Discourse on the Origin and Foundations of Inequality among Men*—asserted that our happiest, original human condition was the so-called state of nature wherein we had not (yet) risen above our mere animal nature. For Rousseau, civilization, the development of our reason, of language, culture, morality, and technology, all signaled our fall from this original blissful natural condition where we were sustained in our own very local environment.

That back-to-nature temptation is not, however, even as modern as Rousseau. Plato treated it directly and deeply in his great philosophical dialogue *The Republic.* The temptation results from a deep recognition that our peculiarly human capacities to reason and to choose freely, which other animals do not share, are precisely the capacities that enable us to bring such great miseries upon ourselves. Better to be rid of them and become just another animal, so the temptation goes, than to be continually beset with the problems that reason and free will bring.

While having great sympathy with this back-to-nature temptation, Plato rejected it, calling a society based upon this view a "city of sows" because it would be built only on what we shared with the other animals: the need for basic bodily sustenance.

For very much the same reason Christians reject this temptation, and in fact everyone who truly desires to follow nature must reject it. Why? Because it's against nature, *our* nature. We are in fact *rational* animals—in Judeo-Christian terms, creatures made in the image of God. We cannot escape our nature, our full nature, but must instead learn to live according to our nature, perfecting our reason and will and desires so that we know, do, and desire what is truly good for us, body and soul, *and* good for the whole pyramid of beings leading up to us on which we depend and for which we must be grateful.

So, we must not be tempted by such a non-answer to our problems. It wouldn't be natural to deny our nature and try to live primitively as if we were just one more animal in our particular ecosystem. That we have the *science* of ecology is as much a part of our natural fulfillment as eating healthy food.

But while science and technology are as natural for us as running at breakneck speed is for a cheetah, that doesn't mean we must embrace a view of science or technology—or morality—that is self-destructive or environmentally destructive. There are not just two alternatives: a society based upon the full-blown primitivism of Rousseau or one based upon the runaway technological mastery of nature for the sake of ever-increasing pleasure, comfort, and entertainment offered by Bacon (which Plato called, centuries in advance, the "feverish city"). Both, in fact, go against our nature, the first by denying it, the second by destroying it in luxurious excess.

The Golden Mean between the Extremes: The Natural Law Culture

There is another sense in which we should go back to nature which avoids both extremes, back to a deeper understanding of nature, including our own nature, that reconnects us to the proper understanding of our full set of potential perfections as human beings, as the rational animal at the top of, and dependent upon, the pyramid of created beings, living as a caring steward over our domain rather than a harsh master. That would be to live in accordance with our nature, in accordance to the natural law.

To live in accordance with the natural law would mean to develop ourselves, our nature, fully, while living within the generous limits of nature and human nature, respecting the integrity of each as giving us boundaries within which to carry on the great adventure of life.

This cannot happen automatically, as if by instinct. We must make the choice in how to live; that is the very essence of our nature as Earth's only moral being, and it is both a privilege and a burden. We can befoul our local ecosystem and pollute others as well. We can harm ourselves by becoming trash-producing, food- and sex-addicted creatures who are a plague on the multiple ecosystems we inhabit, drain energy and resources from, and use as our waste dump. Or, we can take a good hard look at the simple and profound truth that we human beings are part of nature, dependent on the earth's rich ecosystems that form the pyramid of beings underneath us and supporting us. As stewards, rather than tyrants, we can then take care of nature and human nature as if both were great gifts for which we owe the deepest gratitude.

Whether we act in accordance with nature or against it, we are still demonstrating that we are the creature on top of the pyramid who must make rational choices about how to live. Other animals live in an ecosystem and are defined by their own nature within the order of the ecosystem they inhabit. Human beings both live in a particular ecosystem and redefine it, creating a kind of environment that reflects their respective choices, good or bad, in accordance with or against nature and human nature, destructively artificial or salubriously natural.

For shorthand purposes, we may call this matrix of choices by the one term *culture,* and add it to the textbook account of the levels of the ecological hierarchy. A culture is the set of choices, implicit or explicit, that particular human *populations* make about how to live, which are manifested in traditions, characteristic habits and opinions, laws, education, social and political arrangements, clothing, architecture, art, literature, characteristic food production and consumption, pastimes and entertainment, music, dance, as well as religion and general views about nature and human nature. Wherever we find human beings, we find particular cultures, and cultures are a real and natural part of the ecological hierarchy.

But culture is different from the other levels. While certain human populations can live entirely within their own particular *ecosystems,* depending on the living and nonliving resources of the *community* supporting the ecosystem (recall that community includes the water, minerals, soil, plants, and other animals of a particular ecosystem, in our human case, aided by the art of agriculture), it is also natural for human beings to move from one ecosystem to another or travel and trade between *ecosystems* in other *landscapes* or *biomes.*

This is human; it is part of the fulfillment of our nature, and hence the natural law. If for no other reason, this expansion beyond our immediate ecosystem environment is necessary for our being able to gather and trade knowledge about our *biosphere* as a whole and the interactions of the lesser levels of the ecological hierarchy. But this involves a significant amount of economic and technological complexity. Ecologists use all manner of highly sophisticated scientific instruments, as well as cars and planes, to get where they are going in their work. They wear clothes and eat food produced from beyond their home base. They produce books, documentaries, and Internet articles that use a wide variety of resources from multiple levels in the ecological hierarchy, and these are shipped or streamed all over the globe. This is good. We are rational animals by nature, and so science can and should be part of distinct human cultures. It is part of the fulfillment of the natural law.

But we can use our reason and free choice to create cultures that ruin ecosystems, our own and others, by the endless production and consumption of junk and junk food, by the unnatural distortion of sexual desire, or by any of a number of other things. Whatever we choose, it will form a way of life that determines all aspects of our culture accordingly.

A consumerist culture creates habits of excess consumption, a feverish economy that uses massive resources and creates massive waste along with laws to protect and enhance it, education and entertainment aimed at feeding the desire to consume, art and architecture that are cheap, ephemeral, and glitzy, products that are disposable, and a distorted view of human nature to go along with it. Think deeply of the utter foulness of naming human beings "consumers," as if that were indeed our defining trait. That is a culture defined against the natural law.

Or, we can choose a culture defined largely by sexual pleasure, one that redefines any sexual pleasure, no matter how unnatural, as licit. A sex-saturated culture creates pornography that defines the habits and very brains of its inhabitants, and the economy that pushes the culture to ever-greater limits of sexual excess and reaps the profits of what it continually sows, music and dance that mimic the feverish gyrations of uninhibited sexual bacchanalia, art and literature that celebrate every natural sexual boundary broken, education aimed at sexual license and law that supports the aim of that education, and social and political arrangements that destroy the natural family and elevate and legitimate sexual habits previously unknown to biology and human culture both. That is also a culture defined against the natural law.

As we have shown, these are cultures of destruction, both of our nature and nature itself. We have the misfortune of having created a culture that is a union of these two toxic cultures, each side protected by the Right or the Left, respectively. Both violate the natural law, and therefore create a toxic cultural environment. We need a culture based upon the true good of our nature and in accordance with the beneficent order of nature which supports us, one in harmony with the natural law. But that is going to take significant effort on our part, even to see how such a great shift in our culture could occur, as will become clear in the next chapter.

CHAPTER EIGHT

Getting Back to Nature

Nature? What Nature?

A great part of our problem today—for both the Left and the Right—is that we are in a strange condition of being abstracted from nature (including human nature itself) by science and technology. Generally speaking, the Left is abstracted from human nature, and the Right is abstracted from nature. As a result, we have created a culture that keeps us from discovering nature, a culture that deforms human nature from its very earliest stages.

To begin with the obvious, kids today do not play outside and explore nature, but spend almost all their waking hours in day care and school, and playing on computers and smartphones the rest of the time. As a consequence, our kids are hyper-obese *and* they know next to nothing about the natural world. They don't know nature because they were born into a screen culture, which quite literally dominates their landscape. As a result, they live in a virtual, not a natural, world, an artificially created culture that, we must add, is manipulated by the people behind the screens for their great economic profit.[1] This

---

[1] See the brilliant analysis of our screen culture by Matthew Crawford, *The World Beyond Your Head: On Becoming an Individual in an Age of Distraction* (New York: Straus and Giroux, 2015).

kind of abstraction is not limited to our youth, but has become a national habit. Our removal from nature is, largely, a tendency of the Right, and this tendency is amplified by our cultural screen addiction. (To awaken Christians from their slumber in this regard, in staring at our screens we are oblivious to creation, the great and glorious gift of God, and hence to our natural place in that created order.)

But there are less obvious ways in which we have removed ourselves from nature. Ironically, science *itself* has become abstracted from nature, turning away from the study of actual living, breathing, complex things in their environment (a science which used to be called natural history), to the obsessive, reductionist study of the chemical foundations of life, a study done entirely inside, and more and more, on computer screens, thereby compounding the kind of cultural abstraction from nature noted in the previous paragraph. You can't love and care for what you don't know, and our scientists are increasingly alienated from nature itself, from living populations in actual communities in real ecosystems. They've become lab animals themselves, rather than natural historians immersed in the wild. This tendency of science afflicts both the Left and Right.

Even stranger, we have become abstracted from our own natures, including our own *moral* natures (again, the dominant tendency of the Left). We no longer know *what we are*, and hence *what we should be*, and this problem is connected with the other two just mentioned. We have become detached from nature and human nature by our screen culture, and embraced a reductionist view of human nature in science as well, one largely defined by the Baconian notion that our goal in this life is the individual maximization of our bodily pleasure, comfort, and convenience, a goal which demands the mastering of nature (including human nature) by technology for its completion.

For all three reasons, we live in an artificial cultural world, one created by human beings in which nature, seemingly, plays no part (hence, the bite of the parody in the film *Wall-E*). As a consequence of this ignorance, people simply don't care about nature. They don't care about the environment. They don't care about the wonders of creation. They don't even care about their own bodies. They don't care about much of anything but the screen. Again, you can't care about, and care for, what you don't even know.

Let's explore each kind of abstraction and its ill effects, for if we find out how we became detached from nature, including our own nature, then we can more readily figure out how we reattach ourselves again.

The Rebirth of Natural Wonder

The contemporary screen culture isn't entirely new. As a kid, I was largely pulled away from nature by the television and by the endless tedious hours spent (as a very bad investment with no return) inside public school classrooms.

Compared to children today, however, I am a veritable Natty Bumppo (the pioneer protagonist in James Fenimore Cooper's *Leatherstocking Tales*). The culprit is the same but it's become a thousand times worse: the all-absorbing screen devouring children's attention in an increasingly artificial, virtual world, thereby cutting them off from the real, natural world beyond it. The screens today are not just in the corner of one room, like the old television, but everywhere and all day, and as a consequence, the virtual world on the screen largely defines our culture and our worldview. The screen eclipses nature. What does that mean? What can cure it?

The recovery of natural wonder. I still recall the first night that I *saw* the moon. I was, I believe, about 37 or 38 years old. Of course, I knew it was up there all along, although I didn't know much about it. I'd catch a glimpse of it if I happened to be outside at night for a few minutes, but most of my evening time would have been spent staring vacantly at another light, the cyclopean rectangular eye glowing in the living room. The moon was, for me, really like things on the screen: a two-dimensional round object on the blackish backdrop screen of the night sky.

But a strange thing happened one night when I went outside with some binoculars, again, sadly, almost four decades into my life. When I trained them skywards— something I'd never done before—I was overwhelmed, quite literally stunned, because for the first time (with the aid of the binoculars) I saw the moon *as a large, round, real, beautiful, luminous object floating way up in the sky.* I had discovered, late in life, that's what the moon *is*. I stared and stared for I don't know how long.

In this singular experience, I was entirely caught up in what the great ancient philosopher Aristotle called "wonder," the feeling of awe at nature—not a mere sensation, but an overpowering full-body, full-mind, sensuous, and intellectual experience. How can such a thing be, and yet it is! And wonder, as Aristotle goes on to say, is the beginning of philosophy—not an academic discipline in which people are tenured regardless of the merits of their ideas, but according to the etymology of the Greek, the love of wisdom, *philo-sophia*, the natural desire to know the wonder-*full* things in the wise order of nature.

That exhilaration is the primal human experience of our natural world, the one that answers to the deepest and definitive aspects of our rational nature. We are the creatures that can wonder, and inquire into, the wonder-full order of nature. That's what we *should* be doing if we want to experience fully what we really are. That "should," rooted in our deepest nature, has a moral aspect to it, an intrinsic demand for fulfillment that defines the highest aspects of the natural law.

I have looked up into the heavens many times since then, sometimes with the telescope we bought. It is still wonderful, even though I spend too little time doing it, and there is too much artificial light at night where we— and most people—live.

The Cultural Death of Natural Wonder

I had another startling experience in regard to the heavens, this one as dark as the other was light. I'd just gotten done watching some futuristic otherworldly Marvel Comic-type movie with my kids and it suddenly struck me, when I walked outside afterwards and saw the stars, how *boring* the night sky must be to kids who regularly experience (on the screen, through ever more amazing computer graphics,) the thrill of speeding through galaxies past exotic planets. In some computer games they are able to create and destroy imaginary stars, solar systems, and galaxies with a few clicks of a mouse.

So, you point up to the actual night sky for someone immersed in all this hyperpalatable, computer-generated artificiality, and the response is not wonder but a big so-what yawn. It's boring! The actual night sky can't be manipulated. It's just sitting there, a bunch of static dots on a black backdrop. But computer technology on the screen has made us masters of the virtual universe! The Baconian dream fulfilled! On our computers, we gods of the screen can do anything!

Behold, the death of wonder (and I might add, the birth of promethean pride).

If you can do anything on the screen, and the screen is where you spend all your time, then you'll think you can do anything to the things beyond the screen by similar manipulation, especially since so much of our technology in fact is aimed at the manipulation of nature through a screen.

That creates a deeply embedded habit of mind. Reality is ours to do with as we please. The world out there, nature, really doesn't matter, because our fulfillment comes from and through the screen, and the more advanced our technology becomes, the more the world out there can be forced to conform to the virtual realities we create as playgrounds for our pleasure, comfort, and convenience.

Who the heck cares about nature as long as we can plug in our computers or smartphones? Why should we care about the ecosystem within which we live, as long as our hyperpalatable food arrives regularly from elsewhere, and we have a place to plug everything in so we can enjoy our artificial reality?

Nature? What nature? Creation? What creation? How can we care about and care for what we do not know, for what we believe is a far inferior version of something that we can do better through our own technology? And—to goad Christians again—how can we praise God as the all-wise Creator if we implicitly believe that He's second-rate, and that we're actually improving on His first rough draft of reality?

Screen Pollution

The simple answer is "we can't," and so we don't. Instead, our screen culture produces what we may call screen pollution. We remind ourselves from a previous chapter that our new electronics-based culture and economy means the creation of great piles of electronic trash, caused by the continual release of new and improved versions of smartphones, computers, and televisions. Recycling sounds nice, but as we've seen, it actually means the dangerous and pollution-creating sorting of our electronic detritus by the third-world poor so they can salvage usable parts and metals.

That's all bad enough, but there's another kind of screen pollution: the degradation of the human body and mind. Our economy and culture have become based upon screens. And I do not self-righteously exclude myself, since I earn a living, in part, through the very screen upon which I am now watching letters magically arise (and I use the Internet for research).

This takes its toll on our health. Because we've shifted to a screen-based culture, more and more of us make our living sitting for long, long hours staring bleary-eyed at screens. The result: chronic headaches, backaches, obesity, and worse.

Against our nature, we have become the self-destructive, sitting animal. As the new buzz well states it, "Sitting is the new smoking," the new cause of a kind of ill-health

epidemic we've so recently but foolishly visited upon ourselves. Hour after hour of sitting is not natural, a sign of
which is the increased incidence of physical and mental
health problems, such as cardiovascular disease, diabetes, obesity, increased premature mortality, depression,
anxiety, and sleep difficulties among the sedentary.[2] Dr.
James Levine of the Mayo Clinic-Arizona State University
Obesity Solutions Initiative provocatively but accurately
states, "Sitting is more dangerous than smoking, kills more
people than HIV and is more treacherous than parachut-
ing. We are sitting ourselves to death."[3]

If we were looking at any other kind of creature in an
ecosystem with such evident signs of physical distress—
say the population of white-tailed deer were drastically
overweight, limping around on wobbly, nearly-vestigial
legs, bleary-eyed, and uncharacteristically lethargic—we
would look for the causes in changes in the water, air,
foliage, or parasite population to figure out what had gone
wrong in the ecosystem. We don't have that far to look
for the cause of our own evident distress: we have chosen
a screen-based culture, a fairly recent societal, econom-

---

[2]   To see how widespread and recognized the problem is, readers should
do a Google search, "Sitting the new smoking." On the scientific research,
see David Dunstan, Bethany Howard, Genevieve N. Healy, and Neville
Owen, "Too Much Sitting—a Health Hazard," *Diabetes Research and Clin-
ical Practice* 97 (2012): 368–376; Alicia A. Thorp, Neville Owen, Maike
Neuhaus, and David W. Dunstan, "Sedentary Behaviors and Subsequent
Health Outcomes in Adults: A Systematic Review of Longitudinal
Studies, 1996 –2011," *American Journal of Preventive Medicine* 41, no. 2
(2011): 207–215; and Melinda Asztalos, Greet Cardon, Ilse De Bourdeaud-
huij, and Katrien De Cocker, "Cross-Sectional Associations Between
Sitting Time and Several Aspects of Mental Health in Belgian Adults,"
Journal of Physical Activity and Health 12 (2015): 1112–1118.

[3]   Mary MacVean, "'Get Up!' or lose hours of your life every day, scientist
says," *Los Angeles Times,* July 31, 2014, http://www.latimes.com/science/
sciencenow/la-sci-sn-get-up-20140731-story.html.

ic, and cultural choice, which has shown its destructive effects with remarkable rapidity.

Whoops, I Thought We Were Gods

That wasn't how it was supposed to happen. We had a rosy picture of how this technology would turn out, and in many respects it has far exceeded our expectations, but we were woefully shortsighted about the multitude of unexpected harmful effects to nature and human nature of introducing it into our culture. It wasn't something that was added to an existing culture; it devoured and digested the culture.

Now that technology dominates our cultural and our economic ecosystem, our leisure and our work, we find, much to our surprise, that the good comes with considerable and unforeseen ills. Just like the water and air pollution that came with factories that build all the stuff we want and soon throw away; or the poisoning of our water and chronic leaching of the soil that came with large-scale, fertilizer- and pesticide-intensive farming; or the campaign to free sex from any and all restraints.

That lesson in itself is very, very valuable: *human beings tend to be shortsighted smart rather than farseeing wise.* We made a machine to serve us, and it has ended up dominating and defining us instead. We're slaves to our electronic devices, and they are literally sapping the life out of us.

In the deepest respects, this is the unintended result of the Baconian revolution to master nature. In order to master nature, not just in terms of power but wise use as well, we'd need to be all-powerful *and* all-wise. Technology gives us increasingly god-like power, but wisdom is something quite different from scientific-technological power, otherwise we wouldn't so regularly end up harming ourselves and our environment with our newest devices and discoveries.

If the Baconian dream were to be fulfilled, we'd have to be, well, God Himself, all-powerful, wise, and benevolent. But we're not. We're just increasingly powerful human beings with all the nobility and baseness, patience and impulsiveness, refreshing humility and foolish pride, good intentions and wicked designs we've always had. Surprise. Who'd have thunk it? Now we have a screen-based, deformed culture, deforming us in its blinking image.

The Internet Animal

Again, according to the natural law, we are defined by our rationality, our ability to seek out and know the truth. We have become, instead, the Internet animal. As it turns out, the ubiquity of screens has a malforming effect on our own brains, nicely captured in Nicholas Carr's excellent but dismal book, *The Shallows: What the Internet Is Doing to Our Brains.*

Succinctly stated, the Internet as medium is defining our very brains, creating an addiction to a mode of scattered, disjointed, and surface information presentation that quite literally stunts our thinking capacities, harms the defining part of our nature, so that our minds are becoming "rewired" in the distracted, shallow, and impetuous cerebral image of the Internet.

The original article Carr wrote, which formed the seed of his book, even more succinctly states the results of recent research: "Is Google Making Us Stupid?"[4] The answer is yes, or more exactly, the Internet reforms the brain according to its mode of presentation. The continual shallow skimming, consuming of visually hyperpalatable images, hopping around between bits of disconnected information from the glittery surface of a screen (hence, the apt word, "surfing") forms the brain accordingly, making deep thinking and concentration ever more difficult and undesirable. The dopamine rush of the mouse click or swipe ensures a very real addiction, just like lab rats looking for reward hits. Just like cocaine. Just like porn, and hence compounding the bad effects of it.[5] We are becoming less and less capable of real thought. In our immersion on the Internet, Carr explains, "the neural circuits [of the brain] devoted to scanning, skimming, and multitasking are expanding and strengthening, while those used for reading and thinking deeply, with sustained concentration, are weakening and eroding."[6] We are thereby weakening and eroding the very capacities that define us as human. "Dozens of studies by psychologists, neurobiologists, educators, and Web designers point to the same conclusion: when we go online, we enter an *environment* [emphasis added] that promotes cursory reading, hurried and distracted thinking, and superficial learning."[7] The Internet "seizes our attention only to scatter it."[8]

---

4   Nicholas Carr, "Is Google Making Us Stupid? What the Internet Is Doing to Our Brains," *The Atlantic* (July/August 2008).
5   Most research on porn also treats Internet addiction as part of its analysis. See the bibliography in the footnotes to the above chapter on porn for additional research on Internet addiction as a specific kind of addiction. For example, footnote n. 12 on page 105 and others.
6   Nicholas Carr, *The Shallows: What the Internet Is Doing to Our Brains* (New York: Norton, 2010), 141.
7   Ibid., 115–116.
8   Ibid., 118.

I emphasize "environment" as an especially apt word: we are creating an economy, an environment, an artificial ecosystem, a culture that is defined by the Internet, and that environment is stunting our humanity. As the excellent, confessional article by writer-blogger Andrew Sullivan detailing his own struggles with Internet addiction aptly assesses it, "I Used to Be a Human Being."[9]

Immersion in the scattered, obsessive world of the Internet and cell phone culture caused Sullivan's health to deteriorate, his friendships to atrophy, his ability to read books to dissipate, so that his "new way of living was actually becoming a way of not-living."

> Every hour I spent online was not spent in the physical world. Every minute I was engrossed in a virtual interaction I was not involved in a human encounter. Every second absorbed in some trivia was a second less for any form of reflection, or calm, or spirituality. "Multitasking" was a mirage. This was a zero-sum question. I either lived as a voice online or I lived as a human being in the world that humans had lived in since the beginning of time.[10]

Note that Sullivan is actually affirming the reality of the natural law. If our defining feature as human beings is to know truth and live in community with other beings, then of course we'd be miserable if we invented a technology that not only destroyed our minds but also

---

[9] Andrew Sullivan, "I Used to Be a Human Being," *New York Magazine*, September 19, 2016, http://nymag.com/selectall/2016/09/andrew-sullivan-technology-almost-killed-me.html.

[10] Sullivan.

destroyed our friendships with real people.

Realizing these ill effects, do we then give it up? No, says Carr, "We ask the Internet to keep interrupting us, in ever more and different ways. We willingly accept the loss of concentration and focus, the division of our attention and the fragmentation of our thoughts, in return for the wealth of compelling or at least diverting information we receive. Tuning out is not an option many of us would consider."[11]

Why? Because as ample studies have proven since Carr wrote his book, the Internet is addictive—not just metaphorically speaking, but actually addictive, just like certain drugs are addictive, and hence it takes over and defines the lives of its victims. I counted one-hundred and ninety-four books now on Amazon.com dealing, in one way or another, with addiction to the Internet.

The Antidote: The Return to Nature from the World of Screens

Andrew Sullivan did try to beat his addiction, as many others have, by detoxification at a retreat center. Detoxing requires the surrendering of all electronic devices of distraction, and the immersion in nature and the recovery of the depth of the mind. "The task was not to silence everything within my addled brain, but to introduce it to quiet, to perspective, to the fallow spaces I had once known where the mind and soul replenish."[12]

Removing the sources of distractions and immersion

---

[11] Carr, *The Shallows*, 134.
[12] Sullivan.

in nature reawakened in Sullivan the natural attentive wonder that defines human nature—the wonder at creation.

> On a meditative walk through the forest on my second day [of the retreat] I began to notice not just the quality of the autumnal light through the leaves but the splotchy multicolors of the newly fallen, the texture of the lichen on the bark, the way in which tree roots had come to entangle and overcome old stone walls. The immediate impulse—to grab my phone and photograph it—was foiled by an empty pocket. So I simply looked. At one point, I got lost and had to rely on my sense of direction to find my way back. I heard birdsong for the first time in years. Well, of course, I had always heard it, but it had been so long since I listened.[13]

Sullivan's retreat into nature is not an isolated phenomenon. As Eva Selhub and Alan Logan detail in *Your Brain on Nature*, nature therapy (as an alternative to drugs) is beginning to make headway as a scientifically based answer to modernity's techno-frazzled mass culture.[14] Drugs dull or cover up the ill effects; nature restores the natural human health. Japan is leading the way in such nature therapy because, unhappily, they're also leading the way in Internet addiction.[15]

---

[13] Ibid.

[14] Eva Selhub and Alan Logan, *Your Brain on Nature: The Science of Nature's Influence on Your Health, Happiness, and Vitality* (New York: HarperCollins, 2012).

[15] See, for example, Michelle Starr, "Japan to fight Internet addiction with 'fasting camps,'" *CNet*, August 30, 2013, https://www.cnet.com/news/japan-to-fight-Internet-addiction-with-fasting-camps/.

Researchers there have found the immensely beneficial effects of what Japanese call Shinrin-yoku (loosely
translated "forest bathing")—daily immersion in the deep
woods for meditative walks.[16] Studies have found those
who had such walks through the forest had increased
positive feelings, decreased anxiety and depression,
strengthened immune systems, and increased anti-cancer
proteins.[17]

Our need for nature is so powerful and deep that researchers have found that merely having a window that
looks out on a natural setting (onto woods, mountains,
or rural landscapes), as opposed to an urban setting or a
brick wall, decreases the anxiety, the amount of drugs,
and the stay of hospital patients.[18] Not surprisingly,
greener living areas (vs. the concrete and crowded urban
areas) have a significant positive effect in reducing lung,
breast, uterine, prostate, kidney, and colon cancers, and
generally, in reducing the risk of mortality.[19] Having
windows that open on nature in schools and workplaces,
and even putting potted plants indoors, decreases stress

---

[16] E. Morita, et al., "Psychological effects of forest environments on healthy
adults: Shinrin-yoku (forest-air bathing, walking) as a possible method
of stress reduction," *Public Health* 121 (2007): 54–63; Bum-Jin Park, et al.,
"Physiological effects of Shinrin-yoku (taking in the atmosphere of the
forest) in a mixed forest in Shinano Town, Japan," *Scandinavian Journal of
Forest Research* 23 (2008): 278–283; and Yuko Tsunetsugu, Bum-Jin Park,
and Yoshifumi Miyazaki, "Trends in research related to 'Shinrin-yoku'
(taking in the forest atmosphere or forest bathing) in Japan," *Environmental Health and Preventive Medicine* 15 (2010): 27–37.

[17] In addition to the studies noted above, see Selhub and Logan, 18–22.

[18] Roger S. Ulrich, "View through a window may influence recovery from
surgery," *Science* 224, no. 2 (April 1984): 420; and for an expanded analysis with other research akin to this, see Selhub and Logan, *Your Brain on
Nature*, 22–24.

[19] Selhub and Logan, 24–33.

and fatigue, and increases the capacity to concentrate.[20]

In short, immersion in nature—the very thing that those absorbed in screens are denied—is the very thing that cures the ill effects of our screen-addicted culture.[21]

And God Said That It Is Good

To turn the mind and senses to the astounding intricate layers of complexity, harmony, beauty, and peace of creation is to rediscover our proper place as the singular creatures at the top of the great pyramid of beings. We alone can behold the depths and breadth of the order in which we are immersed and upon which we depend with awe, reverence, and understanding—and say, "It is good, very, very good." Even more, contemplation of creation will also make us feel a whole lot better. Think on this liberating thought: we don't have to feel this bad.

But we must recall an important theological reason for surrounding ourselves with a far greener environment, with more trees and less concrete, more woods and less billboards, more parks and less screens. Let us not forget that for Christians nature itself, as the handiwork of the Divine Mind, prepares our minds for God.

Again, St. Paul famously stated at the beginning of his Letter to the Romans, "Ever since the creation of the world his invisible nature, namely, his eternal power and deity, has been clearly perceived in the things that have been made" (Rom 1:20). That means that nature itself—its wise order and beauty—form the foundation of a proof for

---

[20] Ibid., 56–79.
[21] Ibid., chap. 2.

God's existence through natural reason alone.[22] Creation leads us to the Creator.

Surrounding ourselves in the glories of nature is, then, both therapeutic and theological. It would seem, wouldn't it, that Christians would be on the forefront of the preservation of nature and the greening of our cities and suburbs? They should be leading the environmental movement, not ignoring it or churlishly hectoring its proponents. Granted, environmental activists are often misled, in part by a confused desire to worship creation rather than God, in part by a deep antagonism to human beings themselves as spoilers of nature. But if they are misled, then why aren't Christians stepping in to lead them in properly understanding the natural environment? Doing so can be considered an act of compassion for a population increasingly screen-addicted, and hence detached from nature and human nature.

The bad effects of such addiction aren't by any means limited to the stunting of our capacity for deep thinking. I repeat that there is also an explosion of scientific studies on other harmful effects of obsessive Internet use, another deeply obvious sign that something is wrong in our newly-contrived, virtual-based, unnatural culture. The negative effects clinicians and researchers have found among the Internet-addicted are insomnia, depression, suicidal thoughts, obsessive-compulsive behavior, anxiety, substance abuse, aggressive or hostile behavior, social withdrawal, acute family disruption, and failure in school and the workplace. And since the World Wide Web is, as the name trumpets, worldwide, these symptoms plague more and more human

---

[22] See the *Catechism of the Catholic Church*, 31–35.

populations in the entire biosphere.[23]

If someone were purposely causing these destructive symptoms, we would hold him morally responsible and hence blameworthy. But who's to blame, morally, when we are so willing to embrace a technology as part of our human cultural environment that causes so much harm

---

[23] For recent accounts of the vast, worldwide, cross-cultural literature, as well as the diagnosed symptoms of Internet addiction, see Christie Carlisle, et al., "Exploring Internet Addiction as a Process Addiction," *Journal of Mental Health Counseling* 38, no. 2 (April 2016): 170–182; Bülent Baki Telef, "Investigating the Relationship among Internet Addiction, Positive and Negative Effects, and Life Satisfaction in Turkish Adolescents," *International Journal of Progressive Education* 12, no. 1 (2016): 128–135; Kamer Gür, Seher Yurt, Serap Bulduk, and Sinem Atagöz, "Internet addiction and physical and psychosocial behavior problems among rural secondary school students," *Nursing and Health Sciences* 17 (2015): 331–338; Constance C. Milbourn and Jeffrey S. Wilkinson, "When Consumption Becomes All-Consuming in China: The Relationship Between Stickiness and Internet Addiction," *China Media Research* 12, no. 3 (2016): 81–88; Rajshekhar Bipeta, Srinivasa S. R. R. Yerramilli, Ashok Reddy Karredla, and Srinath Gopinath, "Diagnostic Stability of Internet Addiction in Obsessive-compulsive Disorder: Data from a Naturalistic One-year Treatment Study," *Innovations in Clinical Neuroscience* 12, nos. 3–4 (March–April 2015): 14–23; Amandeep Dhir, Sufen Chen, and Marko Nieminen, "Psychometric Validation of Internet Addiction Test With Indian Adolescents," *Journal of Educational Computing Research* 53, no. 1 (2015): 15–31; Agata Błachnio, et al., "Personality and positive orientation in Internet and Facebook addiction. An empirical report from Poland," *Computers in Human Behavior* 59 (2016): 230–236; Agata Błachnio and Aneta Przepiorka, "Association between Facebook addiction, self-esteem and life satisfaction: A cross-sectional study," *Computers in Human Behavior* 55 (2016): 701–705; and Jih-Hsin Tang, et al., "Personality traits, interpersonal relationships, online social support, and Facebook addiction," *Telematics and Informatics* 33 (2016): 102–108; Shahla Ostovar, et al., "Internet addiction and its psychosocial risks (depression, anxiety, stress and loneliness) among Iranian adolescents and young adults: A structural equation model in a cross-sectional study," *International Journal of Mental Health and Addiction* 14 (June 2016): 257–267. This is just a short sample of the vast, very recent worldwide literature. The list goes on and on and on.

to ourselves and the natural environment? We need to become masters rather than slaves of our technology, and that means creating a new culture where technology is at the service of our natural good, that is, the natural law.

Ending Slavery

Just to make sure the lesson is burned into our brains, I'll add one more strand to ensure the deepest seriousness to our inquiries and efforts. Electronic technology, specifically computers and cell phones, depend upon a steady supply of minerals like gold, silver, copper, coltan, and tin. As we've seen in a previous chapter, when we send our junked, obsolete computers and phones to be recycled, they actually end up, for the most part, being dismantled by the poor in other countries so that they can retrieve the various metals for resale.

But the demand can't be met just by such "recycling." Those metals need to be mined. As with the recycling by the world's poor, which is dangerous and done without regard to the environmental consequences, so also with mining: it is often done by what amounts to slaves, working under horrible conditions without any care for what the mining does to either the enslaved or the environment.

Particularly horrifying examples, documented by anti-slavery activist Kevin Bales, are the mines in the Congo, specifically the Bisie mine outside of Walikale. These slaves (men, women, and children) are either captured outright in local villages by thugs and forced to work in the mines, or they are arrested on some trumped up legal charge and compelled to toil in the mines to work off their fines. At Bisie, one finds "a great hollowed-out pile of debris drenched in human waste, toxic chemicals, and blood," surrounding a "mountain of tin [in the form of the ore, cassiterite] and coltan rapidly disappearing as antlike slaves swarm over it and tunnel through it. Twenty thousand people live on this mountain in a city of rags." He continues, "Open pits dot the landscape filled with rainwater and sewage, wriggling with mosquito larvae and parasites. Exhausted, hollow-eyed children, wasted sinewy men, and women with blank stares float through the mist like ghosts and cower when swaggering soldiers pass."[24]

The enormous increase in computer and cell phone use since the 1980s had an obvious economic effect: skyrocketing economic demand meant, in turn, just as great a demand for the raw materials, especially metals, including the tin that's used for soldering electronics. Villagers in the Congo found they could increase their livelihood by picking up cassiterite pebbles exposed around the Bisie mountain and selling them. But brutal soldiers, who were produced by the Congo Wars, realized they could make a lot of money by forcing villagers to gather and mine cassiterite for them. Now men and boys burrow through the mines. "Women and girls tend to be used for cleaning the ore, for cooking, or for sex."[25] Since slavers don't care about what happens to slaves, those in the mine soon develop silicosis, "which occurs when the lungs fill with microscopic sharp-edged rock dust. The dust makes the lungs bleed and form scar tissue. As the scar tissue expands, the lungs can't bring oxygen to the body. In time even an otherwise

---

[24] Kevin Bales, *Blood and Earth: Modern Slavery, Ecocide, and the Secret to Saving the World* (New York: Spiegel & Grau, 2016), 47.

[25] Ibid., 48–49.

healthy person withers away, slowly but irreversibly suffocating to death. Flying shards of rock from the chisels regularly damage eyes, and rock falls and other accidents break bones."[26] The mining camps are rife with disease; death comes early and often.

The minerals from these death camps are sold by the slavers to the mineral dealers in the Congo, who then sell it to the exporters. They in turn sell the minerals to the big companies who further process the metals so they are fit for use in our electronics, and then sell these refined metals to manufacturers of the electronics, who then ship them to stores which sell them to us.[27] Just so you don't think the only maltreatment of workers is in the mines, investigation has revealed the miserable conditions of those who put the cell phones together, Apple being one of the worst.[28]

That's the economic chain that brings computers to our desks and cell phones to our pockets. By the time it gets to us, we may or may not have a device whose metals originated in a slave mine such as Bisie; perhaps they came from a well-regulated mining operation that cared for the workers and the environment. We don't know. We don't really even think about it.

---

[26] Ibid., 49.

[27] Ibid., 52–64.

[28] George Knowles, "Inside the eerie deserted dorms where Apple iPhone workers lived eight to a room, showered in groups of 20 and even PAID for the privilege," *The Daily Mail*, May 11, 2016, http://www.dailymail. co.uk/news/article-3582640/Open-sewers-mildewed-walls-one-toilet-FORTY-people-Shocking-pictures-dirty-dormitories-Apple-s-iPhone-workers-live-like-animals.html.

Saving Our Nature from Screen Pollution

Shall we then destroy all this new screen technology and throw ourselves back into the most primitive animal existence? Shall we try to follow Rousseau and shed our human rational nature? The answer is a most emphatic no. But we also don't have to live in what Plato called the "feverish city"—in our case, in a culture defined by the hyperpalatable virtual world.

We need to aim at a middle ground, between indiscriminately throwing out all our technology, or indiscriminately embracing it—thereby becoming slaves to the machines we've made. To do so we must recall ancient wisdom about human nature which is an essential aspect of the natural law: we should seek, first of all, to master ourselves, to master our passions and desires, to moderate them by recovering the forgotten virtue of temperance.

self-mastery and temperance

Our human nature is meant for deeper things than frittering away our time in virtual reality and losing our mental and physical health in the process, scattering our souls and our lives into billions of pixels and millions of disconnected moments. We need to create a culture that reconnects us to the depths of reality, of nature, and especially our own nature, where technology is a mere instrument for this more noble goal, rather than a harsh master who drives us away from our own health and happiness.

yesss!

We mustn't think, however, that our omnipresent screens are the only thing removing us from nature. Ironically, our natural scientists themselves are—could anything be stranger?—increasingly detached from nature.

The Death of Nature in Science

It is beyond strange to report—and the report comes from an increasing number of disgruntled scientists— that our newest generation of scientists knows very little about nature at all, that is, actual nature: birds, trees, turtles, swans, giraffes, wild pigs, rattlesnakes, actual eco-systems. The reason is not a surprise, given the previous section. The new generation of biologists has not only grown up on screens, but also they have been trained in a reductionist view of science, one that disregards actual living creatures swarming in real ecosystems, and focuses instead on the chemical foundations of life as manipulated in the lab and in models of ecosystems and populations on the computer.

Scientists used to be naturalists, studying actual living things, becoming experts in birds, trees, fish, snakes, grasses, and their place in real ecosystems. This scientific approach to deep immersion in nature was the standard. As I noted above, it was called by that delightfully old-fashioned name, natural history. But as butterfly expert (lepidopterist) Robert Michael Pyle laments, this approach is becoming increasingly rare, and perhaps approaching extinction.[29]

As Pyle reports, colleges and universities in his youth had "a plethora of natural history classes: birds, mammals, insects, local flora, lichens and mosses, mushrooms, marine invertebrates, paleontology, astronomy, on and

---

[29] Robert Michael Pyle, "The Rise and Fall of Natural History," *Orion* (Autumn 2001): 17–23. For a similar, more detailed account of the "fall of natural science" see David Schmidly, "What It Means to Be a Naturalist and the Future of Natural History at American Universities," *Journal of Mammalogy* 86, no. 3 (2005): 449–456.

on."[30] These were not book classes, but *field* classes, actual get-out-in-the-real-world-and-explore-nature-with-an-expert classes.

But sometime about the mid-twentieth century, the "old-style" natural historians were shuffled off the academic stage. Departments wanted instead "superstar lab candidates" for academic positions "who published frequently in all the right journals." But these new lab scientists were microbiologists rather than macrobiologists, and so "had little connection with the field." Consequently, natural history courses that immersed students in nature were replaced by lab courses increasingly focused on computers. Thus, "the attrition of academic naturalists has been progressive over the past half-century."[31]

This is not a vague conjecture of an isolated and grumpy naturalist, but is verifiable (as shown by Joshua Tewksbury, et al.) in a breakdown of the Ph.D.s in biology in the United States during the latter half of the twentieth century. Doctorates in biology rose from under two thousand to over seven thousand. Good news, right? But when we look at the breakdown by subdiscipline, we find that the doctorates received in natural history-related disciplines plummeted downward, cut in half during this time, while microbiology and molecular biology doctorates shot upward. In the 1950s, all college biology majors had to take natural history courses, and the natural history approach dominated the textbooks used. College kids studied actual animals, plants, birds, and fish in their ecosystems. "Today, the majority of universities and colleges in the United States have no natural history requirements

---

[30] Pyle, 17.
[31] Ibid., 18.

for a degree in biology, and the emphasis on natural history in introductory biology texts has dropped 40 percent over the past 50 years."[32] Look at almost any college or high school biology textbook and I will guarantee that the first three-quarters of the book will be focused on biochemistry, followed up by a few, cursory chapters on plants and animals as a kind of intellectual afterthought.

Scientific training in biology without any connection to nature. Deep knowledge of the organism in its environment academically and scientifically passé. A rather ironic result, isn't it? Training in statistics and computer manipulations—the abstract treatment of species populations—has become the intellectual standard. The result, as M. A. Mares bluntly states, is that young biologists "are sublimely ignorant of the diversity and complexity of nature."[33]

The odd situation created by this transformation of our science of nature, according to Pyle, was that these now-dominant "lab scientists frequently knew next to nothing about the organisms they studied as molecular and cellular 'systems' or mathematical models. . . ." The reductionist approach "helped to drive research away from the whole organism and into the cell and the molecule, thus out of the field and into the lab. Natural history was [thereby] placed on a high, dusty shelf as a romantic artifact."[34] Studying real fish, birds, reptiles, and mammals in their actual ecosystem habitat—how quaint!

The result, as noted conservation biologist Reed Noss states, is that "The naturalists are dying off and have few

---

[32] Joshua Tewksbury, et al., "Natural History's Place in Science and Society," *BioScience* 64, no. 4 (April 2014): 300–310; data and quotes from 304–305.

[33] Quoted in Schmidly, 452.

[34] Pyle, 21.

heirs." He continues, "Our sophisticated technological tools can . . . be good things (though I am ambivalent on this point) to the extent that they enable us to make better maps of the patterns of nature and more accurate predictions of the responses of biological elements to potential futures. But I cannot help feeling uneasy in the knowledge that the middle-aged biologists of today . . ."—the article was written two decades ago, so they are now near retirement—". . . may be the last generation to have been exposed to truly wild places and to have been taught serious natural history as part of their professional training."[35] Warns Noss accordingly, "*Scientific abstraction and fancy technologies are no substitutes for the wisdom that springs from knowing the world and its creatures in intimate, loving detail. . . .* Without years of bug-bitten trudging through hollows and bogs, how can a biologist be expected to be able to separate biological truth from computer fabrication?" (emphasis added).[36]

This academic abstraction from nature both mirrors and reinforces the larger, above-mentioned abstraction from nature in our culture where children are absorbed in screens rather than playing in and studying nature. The pre-screen, pre-reductionist approach used to define our life and the education about nature that our youth would receive. Kids used to know their local ecosystems by immersion and education. As Pyle notes,

> Nature study premised itself on the assumption that boys and girls would become acquainted with

---

[35] Reed Noss, "The Naturalists are Dying off," *Conservation Biology* 10, no. 1 (February 1996): 1–3.

[36] Ibid., 2.

their local flora and fauna by name, features, and habit. What birds flew and nested near the school, and how did they feed? What plants sprang up, outside the garden? Who sang in the spring chorus at dusk? But today, I see students coming out of school with no appreciable knowledge of their nonhuman neighbors: every evergreen is a pine, all brown birds are sparrows; and if a spring chorus is to be heard at all, a frog is a frog is a frog.[37]

Our children are addicted to screens and surrounded by concrete, wallboard, carpet, and fluorescent lights, and so have no real, particular knowledge of nature—only a tepid grasp on general names. But are we adults any better? Can you name more than three or four birds in your local surroundings?

The harm is, again, that we can't love what we don't know, and the deeper we know it, the deeper our love. This is as true for other people as it is for other animals, and plants, and stars, and all the wonderful things existing beyond the screen. "Ecological ignorance breeds indifference, throttling up the cycle I call the extinction of experience," explains Pyle.[38] Since we don't spend our time among real, natural creatures and ecosystems, we have no real, sustained experience of them, so we don't care what happens to them. Woodlands, fields, trees, flowers, creeks and cricks, wetlands and their multitude of denizens disappear under a layer of concrete or behind a mini-mall or billboard, and we scarcely look up from our screens to notice. So, "as common elements of [ecological] diver-

---

[37] Pyle, 22.
[38] Ibid., 18.

sity disappear from our own nearby environs, we grow increasingly alienated, less caring, more apathetic. Such collective anomie allows further extinctions and deeper impoverishment of experience, round and round. What we know, we may choose to care for. What we fail to recognize, we certainly won't."[39]

Noss concurs: "Empathy for living things comes from many years of observing them in their natural environments, which is why field biologists have always been among the most adamant defenders of wild Nature." We therefore must resist the "trend toward indoor biology" that now defines almost all academic biological training today, in high schools, colleges, and graduate schools, and instead demand that curricula on all levels reinstate real field biology, because "conservation biology is fundamentally about real organisms in real environments."[40] As ecologists David Wilcove and Thomas Eisner put it in their article "The Impending Extinction of Natural History," "The deinstitutionalization of natural history looms as one of the biggest scientific mistakes of our time, perpetrated by the very scientists and institutions that depend upon natural history for their well-being."[41]

This "deinstitutionalization," we must remind ourselves, did not happen in historical or cultural isolation. It was the result of accepting the reductionist, materialist Baconian-Cartesian view of nature that assumes that living, diverse organisms are actually only epiphenomena of subvisible atomic reality. On this reductionist

---

[39] Ibid., 18.

[40] Noss, 2.

[41] David Wilcove and Thomas Eisner, "The Impending Extinction of Natural History," *Chronicle of Higher Education* 47 (September, 2000): B24.

approach to science, the point is not to know the "epiphenomena," real living things, but to reduce them to their microscopic foundations, so that we can better learn to manipulate and reconstruct them according to our own purposes. The secular project of mastering nature for this-worldly pleasure means that nature is seen as raw material for our designs in creating a better version of our world, an artificial world that better fits our desires, our pleasures, our comforts, and our insatiable passion for amusement.

The benefits of turning once again to nature would be immense. Reinstating natural history—the sustained study of real, living beings in their natural environment, contemplating deeply what they actually are and what they actually do—simultaneously cures us of our societal hyper-addiction to the screen and immerses us in nature to discover, once again, what it means to wonder. When I say "reinstating" I mean not just in academia but in our daily lives. Science understood as natural history reattaches us to the very depths of our human nature, since the entire pyramid of nature beneath us quite literally constitutes us and sustains us, and we are engaging in the very activity of knowing, the activity that defines our place at the top of that pyramid.

Reinstating natural history in science will demand—and isn't this ironic—that we push screen- and lab-addicted scientists, especially biologists, out into the wild for significant *nature therapy*. They need to understand that the reductionist approach to nature is the wrong approach to science, a sign of this being that scientists are increasingly abstracted from real nature, nature as it presents itself to the mind and the senses of human beings, nature as it is so wonderfully lived in actual, living ecosystems.

This would demand a much different understanding of how science is done and how nature must be understood that would, quite literally, turn reductionism upside down—or, since it is a corrective, right-side up. As noted in a previous chapter, nature is not homogeneous but complex and diverse. The natural hierarchies we discussed—atoms, molecules, cells, tissues, organs, organ systems, organisms, populations, communities, ecosystems, landscapes, biomes, and the biosphere—are nested hierarchies, where (as ecologists Eugene Odum and Gary Barrett explain) "each level is made up of groups of lower-level units (populations are composed of organisms, for example)." They continue,

An important consequence of hierarchical organization [in biology] is that as components, or subsets, are combined to produce larger functional wholes, new properties emerge that were not present at the level below. Accordingly, an **emergent property** of an ecological level or unit cannot be predicted from the study of the components of that level or unit. Another way to express the same concept is **non-reducible property**— that is, a property of the whole not reducible to the sum of the properties of the parts. Though findings at any one level aid in the study of the next [higher] level, they never completely explain the phenomena occurring on the next level, which must be studied to complete the picture.[42]

---

[42] Odum and Barrett, 7. This holistic ecological approach is supported by (but not reducible to) the anti-reductionist approach of systems biology. See the historical summary of the development of the holistic, anti-reductionist approach of systems biology by Srdjan Kesic, "Systems

This emergent approach obviously goes against the grain of our current reductionist view which collapses the higher levels of organisms, populations, communities, and ecosystems into the lowest levels of atoms, molecules, and cells. By contrast, the emergent approach assumes that the non-reducible properties of each distinct ecological level in the ecological hierarchy have their own integrity and must be studied on the level of their emergence. You can't deduce organisms or ecosystems from atoms. While there are what Odum and Barrett call "collective properties" (that is, properties on higher levels which "are summations of the behavior of components" on lesser levels of the ecological hierarchy), the emergent properties of the higher levels, the levels of life, must be studied on their own terms.

That doesn't mean we do away with microbiology; rather, microbiology, macrobiology, and ecology work hand in hand. "Each biosystem level has emergent properties . . . as well as a summation of attributes of its subsystem components [i.e., collective properties]."[43] An elk or an elephant is indeed made up of atoms, molecules, cells, organs, and organ systems, but it also has its own emergent properties as a whole, living organism, and further properties emerge as parts of a population herd within an ecosystem community of other animals, birds, plants, etc. Reducing biology to microbiology, and microbiology to chemistry, is causing the death of natural history. Our science of nature must be aimed at all levels because emer-

---

biology, emergence and antireductionism," *Saudi Journal of Biological Sciences* 23 (2016): 584–591. Also, on the more general struggle between reductionists and anti-reductionists historically, see Massimo Pigliucci, "Between holism and reductionism: a philosophical primer on emergence," *Biological Journal of the Linnean Society* 112 (2014): 261–267.

[43] Ibid., 8.

gent properties cannot be predicted; they must be studied first hand. Natural history isn't optional and hence obsolete; science is stunted if it remains in the reductionist rut. "The folk wisdom about the forest being more than just a collection of trees is, indeed, a first working principle of ecology."[44] Scientists cannot remain abstracted from living things in real ecosystems and remain true scientists. And if we are not true scientists, we are acting against our nature as knowers. Knowing nature as it really is, in all its luxuriant beauty and diversity, is part of the perfection of our rational nature, as the natural law rightly states.

We are, by this reflection, brought to our third sense in which we have become abstracted from our own nature, one that builds on the first two: the abstraction from our own nature.

The Eclipse of Human Nature

If we have become increasingly abstracted from nature, both in our daily screen-saturated life and in the very science of biology, then it would seem very likely that we've become similarly abstracted from human nature. Immersed in our virtual world, we have lost our own nature and have thereby become increasingly dehumanized.

We've already seen, in significant part, how this has happened. Once we defined ourselves as entirely material, pleasure-seeking creatures with nothing to live for but maximizing our bodily pleasures and minimizing our pains through technological mastery of nature, we began to see nature as something to be manipulated for the sake of this

---

[44] Ibid.

hedonistic goal rather than a wonder-full order with its own complex integrity that must be studied and respected.

But of course, the same thing happened to our own nature. Given our Baconian utilitarian goal, we began to see *human nature* as something to be manipulated for the sake of this hedonistic goal, rather than a wonder-full order with its own complex integrity that must be respected.

Our super-destructive addiction to Internet pornography is only the most obvious example of our embrace of the most intense, individual sensual pleasure, one that pollutes our human sexual nature and the sexual nature of others by treating them as raw material for our ever more raw obsessions—as if we, among all the animals, could do whatever we wanted with sexuality, regardless of the intrinsic biological and moral realities of our nature. We are increasingly absorbed into screen sex, and don't care what happens, no matter how destructive to nature, to ourselves, or to anyone else.

We must therefore think about the obvious—and here I am aware that I'm now goading the Left just as hard as I was previously goading the Right in regard to environmental pollution. If we can't do whatever we want for our own private pleasure in regard to the natural environment, in regard to the water, the forests, the atmosphere, the fields, or in regard to other species—whether cuttlefish or caribou, woodpeckers or salmon—how can it be that we believe that we should be able to do whatever we want with our own sexual nature? Isn't our own human sexuality part of our ecology? Isn't human sexual nature part of nature? Isn't a non-toxic cultural environment devoid of sex pollution the most healthy environment?

If we, in virtue of being at the top of the biological pyramid, have a moral duty to take care of the natural

world—the rest of the pyramid, upon which we depend—
don't we have a moral duty to care for the integrity of our
own sexual nature?

But we can't and won't if—as has become the case in
regard to nature in general over the last few decades—
we've become increasingly abstracted from our own sexual
nature. As with our abstraction from the natural world,
we can't rediscover our own sexual nature if our attitude
is "we want what we want and damn the consequences."

This is not a mere negative shaming, but an invitation
to discovery. As with recovering our proper wonder at the
natural world, we also might discover—if we could turn
our attention to our sexual nature, rather than turn to pornography for its manipulation—that it is also wonder-full.

I begin with the obvious: male and female are natural
distinctions. We are animals defined fundamentally by
our capacities to procreate, but that is nothing peculiar
to human beings. So is just about every other creeping,
crawling, running, flying, swimming creature out there.
Biologically, reproduction is an essential part of animal
nature. That's how it is throughout nature. How could it
be otherwise with us?

But we have become masters of manipulation of our
reproductive biology, our sexuality, even our gender.
The beginning of our abstraction from our sexual nature
was not Internet porn. As I indicated above, it was the
development of the Pill because—true to its Baconian in-
spiration of mastering nature for the sake of pleasure—it
technologically cut sexual pleasure from its natural biological aim in the same way that we've removed sweetness
from actual health-giving food. It did so not just for the
individuals involved, but for our society.

The result is that Pill came to define our sexual

culture just as thoroughly as the Internet. In our society, purposely breaking that connection between sexual pleasure and biological aim, sexual pleasure became the defining goal, and soon enough, the all-consuming goal. Other people became a means to that end, instruments of ever more feverish pursuits of pleasure, regardless of the ill effects. In particular, women have become the instruments for men who have no anxiety about using them and then discarding them—no biological, emotional, or marital strings attached. The Pill cut the biological strings, and enabled the consequent abstraction from this natural foundation, and thereby cut the emotional and marital strings as well.

Since the introduction of the Pill in the mid-twentieth century, marital rates have plummeted, transient cohabitation has risen (along with divorce), and sexuality has become entirely untethered from natural gender, and in fact, gender itself has been expanded to categories beyond counting. Facebook currently offers users fifty-six gender options, virtually endless categories for those addictively immersed in its virtual world, where you can be anyone you want with countless "friends" you'll never meet in person.[45]

This virtual "reality" existence mirrors the fate of sex itself in society. What originally brought male and female together in a union of love for the sake of offspring, just like every other animal, is now defined largely by the solitary masturbation of an individual locked in his room, glued to the screen. The most social act, the sexual act that

---

45 Will Oremus, "Here Are All the Different Genders You Can Be on Facebook," Slate, February 13, 2014, http://www.slate.com/blogs/future_tense/2014/02/13/facebook_custom_gender_options_here_are_all_56_custom_options.html.

creates the family, has now become a solitary, loveless, and narcissistic act. What if an alien biologist suddenly landed on earth? What would he conclude had happened to this one particular species?

Note again how, as with the Internet itself, this malformation violates our essential nature, the natural law: our nature is made to be social, we are made for community, and sexuality is made for the most intimate of all communities, the union of male and female in the deepest friendship. But we have become sexually asocial, or even anti-social.

As documented in the depressing but enlightening *Man (Dis)connected* by Philip Zimbardo and Nikita Coulombe, men increasingly prefer virtual sex with pixelated women over actual biological sex with real women.[46] Even visits to flesh-and-blood prostitutes are becoming obsolete with the advent of "virtual escort" services. In the wildly popular, aptly named Massively Multiplayer Online Role Playing Game *Second Life* (which absorbs the "first," actual lives of its players, into its virtual world), there is a Red-Light District (reports author and former Internet addict, Andrew Doan) "with virtual escorts, strip bars, and genitalia attachments in order to experience virtual sex." The women behind the on-screen avatars sometimes can make six-figure incomes.[47] The hyperpalatable masturbatory virtual-world experience, with no emotional, psychological, economic, moral, or marital strings attached, trumps old-fashioned

---

[46] Philip Zimbardo and Nikita Coulombe, *Man (Dis)connected: How Technology Has Sabotaged What It Means to Be Male* (London: Rider, 2015), 13, 18, 90, 194–196.

[47] Andrew Doan, *Hooked on Games: The Lure and Cost of Video Game and Internet Addiction* (Coralville, LA: F.E.P. International, Inc., 2012), 87–88.

biological sex between an actual male and female.[48]

The ultimate abstraction via technology, from our sexual natures, from the depth of our biological maleness and femaleness, is especially degrading for women. Women are increasingly being replaced by sexbots, which are just what you think they are: machines made in the image of a woman but entirely for the sexual pleasure of men.[49] That's all the new solitary male wants. Real women aren't worth the bother. How far removed is that from nature?

Strange to say it, but the Pill, which started the whole sexual revolution technologically, *is fast becoming as obsolete as the women who used to take it.* Why take the Pill if actual men aren't interested in actual sex, but prefer compliant artificial machines to actual women? What has happened to maleness that it prefers a machine to a soulmate and friend? Men are becoming increasingly abstracted not only from real women, but their own nature as well.

The collapse in maleness is becoming increasingly widespread. Porn isn't the only problem. As Zimbardo and

---

[48] Zimbardo and Coulombe, 107–119.

[49] Eva Wiseman, "Sex, love, and robots: Is this the end of intimacy?" *The Guardian*, December 13, 2015, https://www.theguardian.com/technology/2015/dec/13/sex-love-and-robots-the-end-of-intimacy. There are endless other articles on the Internet (as well as the websites for the rising number of companies rushing into this economically inviting opportunity). See, for example, MILO, "Sexbots: Why Women Should Panic," *Breitbart*, September 16, 2015, http://www.breitbart.com/big-government/2015/09/16/sexbots-why-women-should-panic/; Catharine Smith, "The Rise Of The Sex Machines: Inside The Future Of Sexbots," *The Huffington Post*, November 28, 2012, http://www.huffingtonpost.com/2012/11/28/the-rise-of-the-sex-machines-roxxxy-sexbot_n_2207584.html; and George Gurley, "Is This the Dawn of the Sexbots?" *Vanity Fair*, May 2015, http://www.vanityfair.com/culture/2015/04/sexbots-realdoll-sex-toys.

Coulombe make clear, it's also addictive Internet gaming—or, more often, a combination of the two. Boys are no longer becoming men, but rather remain in their parents' basements, with no interest in real women or the real world, thereby becoming self-absorbed, emasculated parodies of manhood locked bug-eyed in their rooms. They were given video games as little boys and never stopped playing them. As deformed little man-boys, they have no desire to be a real man and work to support a family. Mommy and daddy, if there is a daddy, will always cook and clean for them, pay their bills, and buy them what they need.[50]

As recent research has shown, young men are "rejecting work" because "they have a better alternative: living at home and enjoying video games." This rise in basement boys parallels the tripling in their screen time. One of the chief reasons—think about this, please—is the "increasingly sophisticated video games are luring young men away from the workforce."[51] It's just so much more interesting and easy than reality. In the hyperpalatable virtual world a man-boy can be anything, effortlessly conquering worlds and women all day and night. By contrast, real life takes work. Real women demand sacrifice and love. The effects are measurable and miserable. "In 2014, for the first time in more than 130 years," Pew Research reports, "adults ages 18 to 34 were slightly more likely to be living in their parents' home than they were to be living with a spouse

---

[50] Zimbardo and Coulombe, chaps. 1–4.

[51] Ana Swanson, "Why amazing video games could be causing a big problem for America," Washington Post, September 23, 2016, https://www.washingtonpost.com/news/wonk/wp/2016/09/23/why-amazing-video-games-could-be-causing-a-big-problem-for-america/?postshare=4741474661762783&tid=ss_fb.

or partner in their own household."[52] An amazing statistic! Marriage and now even living together are becoming passé!

The US isn't the only one suffering shrinking maleness. Japan and China, both super-screen absorbed, are having the same problem, but to a greater extent. An increasing number of men have no interest in actual sex, both non-married and married, not because they've lost their libido, but because they are lost in the hyperpalatable virtual gaming and porn world.

In Japan, they are called *soshoku danshi*, herbivorous men, rather than carnivorous men who still seek real woman. In China, they are called *diaosi*, which I won't translate, so as to avoid embarrassment. These are the men who may work, but so entirely lack social skills because of their intense addiction to gaming that they never do anything else—a vicious circle that drives them to play video games in isolation because they are so socially inept.[53]

This kind of social isolation in virtual reality is becoming epidemic. In Japan, the chronic shut-in phenomenon is called *hikikomori*, and according to a recent survey, "541,000 15 to 39-year-olds were living in isolation. . . . those who have shut themselves in their homes for at least seven years accounted for 35 percent of the total. Another 29 percent have lived as recluses for three to five years . . ." These shut-ins, primarily men, are so self-isolated that they only communicate with others through the Internet—even

---

[52] Richard Fry, "For First Time in Modern Era, Living With Parents Edges Out Other Living Arrangements for 18- to 34-Year-Olds," *Pew Research Center*, May 24, 2016, http://www.pewsocialtrends.org/2016/05/24/for-first-time-in-modern-era-living-with-parents-edges-out-other-living-arrangements-for-18-to-34-year-olds/.

[53] Zimbardo and Coulombe, 18.

those who are in the same house. Like little boys, they play video games and read comics.[54]

A collapse of manhood into hollow-eyed, self-absorbed, miserably lonely blobs behind computer screens. A collapse of women in despair who've given up on blob-men because blob-men just want porn or sexbots because actual women (not to mention marriage and kids) are too much trouble. The cultural transformation of loving, caring men into libidinous creatures who want girlfriends and wives to act like porn stars or sexbots, and who soon give up real for virtual sex. The extinction of actual, real, biological, intimate, loving sexual intercourse using one's actual parts for their obvious biologically-defined functions, its place taken by an increasingly raw list of ever more violent, sadistic, abusive, dangerous, and entirely unbiological sexual activity—a collapse lamented even by some of those who so fervently advocate the unnatural pleasures causing the extinction.[55]

Is There a Cure?

We have some serious questions to ask ourselves. How have we become so abstracted from our biological nature at the most rudimentary level that we believe that male

---

[54] Fabiola Sarchione, et al., "Hikikomori: clinical and psychopathological issues," *Research and Advances in Psychiatry* 2, no. 1 (2015): 21–27. See also Harriet Agerholm, "Half a million young people in Japan barely leave their homes," *Independent*, September 26, 2016, http://www.independent.co.uk/news/world/asia/young-people-japan-hikikomori-anxiety-a7329396.html.

[55] A prime case being the raunchy Rebecca Reid, "Have we forgotten how to have 'normal' sex?" *The Telegraph*, May 27, 2016, http://www.telegraph.co.uk/women/sex/the-death-of-vanilla-sex-how-britain-got-raunchy/.

and female are optional biological categories for us, especially when we, as students of nature, don't treat any other animal that way? How could male and female be optional for the human animal alone, and moreover, subject to endless Baconian hedonistic and technological manipulation?

What if, exhausted by the unnatural state of our sexual lives, as exhausted as Andrew Sullivan was by his lonely virtual blog life, we shed our techno-enhanced, screen-based, hyperpalatable porno-utopianism and took a walk back into human nature, a walk to restore our natural sexual selves. What might we find?

We might find, once the gibbering clamor for sensual hyperstimulation began to subside, that male and female are—*by* and *in* nature—meant to be the deepest of friends, quite literally made for each other to create a union of love in which mutually complementary biological sexuality, as wonder-full as it is, points to something even deeper that answers to the fullness of our nature as rational animals, to our particular senses, heart, mind, and soul. We might find that our biologically complementary sexuality points to the deepest friendship of two becoming one, who then cannot live without each other and so live for each other, a union of two in one flesh that naturally brings forth a new living being, one out of the two, who also must be loved, and must also be taught to care for all of nature in the great pyramid of beings that makes this, and all life, possible.

We are, I repeat, meant *by nature* for this deepest of friendships because we are *social* by nature. As the natural law states, we are "political animals," meaning by this not that we are obsessed with politics, but that we are made to live together in mutually-supporting and enriching communities, beginning with the biological family. If we could put it in biblical terms, man was not meant to be alone, and so woman was created, each made for the other in a complementary union.

It isn't all about sex, I remind the reader. The same continual saturation in virtual reality that is killing our sexual nature is killing our social nature, as just noted. But it's also killing our rational nature because we are too frittered by screen absorption to think deeply about anything, including, especially, the beautiful order of nature. That's an unpleasantly comprehensive ruination of our human nature, a real pollution destroying what we should be. And again, if we pollute ourselves, why should we care whether we pollute the environment?

Too Many Bad Coincidences

Here's an important intellectual and moral exercise for both the Left and Right. On one timeline, each of you graph the kind of degradation that most concerns you. Note that the precipitous increase in both environmental and moral degradation map onto each other fairly closely, rising slowly but surely in the last part of the nineteenth century, and jetting dizzyingly upwards at about the mid-twentieth century. The same is true for the topics we've addressed in this chapter. The cultural domination of television, computers, the Internet, and then smartphones begins at about the mid-twentieth century, as does the dominance of the reductionist approach to science that jettisons natural history, and the technological manipulation of our sexuality, beginning with the Pill and ending with porn and sexbots. If we add to all of this the graph of the social and moral breakdown of the natural family since the 1950s, we see all too clearly the poisoned fruits of the Baconian attempt to master nature for our own individual pleasure (rather than, as the natural law would have it, to live a life of virtue according to the limits of nature and human nature).

I am not, I stress, arguing that all of our problems could be solved if we only went back to the good old days of the 1940s. The Baconian revolution has been going on for several centuries, long before the precipitous rise of the negative consequences in the twentieth and now twenty-first century of working according to its assumptions. Bad ideas take time to filter down culturally, and since these bad ideas entailed significant technological advancements, the promised "victory" of the mastery over nature had to wait until the technology was developed. Now we are living in the midst of (to recall Pope Francis' words) the tyranny of the "technocratic paradigm."[56] We have mastered nature by technology, and our technology has mastered us. "The idea of promoting a different cultural paradigm and employing technology as a mere instrument" as the natural law would have it "is nowadays inconceivable," laments Pope Francis.

> It has become countercultural to choose a lifestyle whose goals are even partly independent of technology, of its costs and its power to globalize and make us all the same. Technology tends to absorb everything into its ironclad logic, and those who are surrounded with technology "know full well

---

[56] *Laudato si'*, §§106–114.

that it moves forward in the final analysis neither for profit nor for the well-being of the human race," that "in the most radical sense of the term power is its motive—a lordship over all." As a result, "man seizes hold of the naked elements of both nature and human nature."[57]

Needless to say, in pointing out the problems in our increasing acceptance of our own machines lording it over us, creating our culture, our bodies, our sexuality, and our brains in their image, Pope Francis is simultaneously calling us to freedom from these self-created shackles. "There needs to be a distinctive way of looking at things, a way of thinking, policies, an educational programme, a lifestyle and a spirituality which together generate resistance to the assault of the technocratic paradigm."[58]

It is not the pope's intention—nor is it mine—to argue that we need to do away with technology. Again, our nature is defined by rationality, and technology is an aspect of our rational nature. What we must aim for is not the elimination of technology in some kind of romantic Rousseau-like reaction, but the self-conscious, wise subordination of technology to the good of our nature and the integrity of the natural environment. We shouldn't be defining ourselves or our culture by cell phones and screens. We are better than that. Our nature and nature itself are far more wonderful than the artificial world that steals so much of our time, and ends up leaving us feeling alone, miserable, and, frankly, a whole lot more stupid. We need to have real friends rather than piling up Facebook friends,

---

[57] Ibid., §108.
[58] Ibid., §111.

real encounters of wonder with the cornucopia of creatures inhabiting our local ecospheres, real culture built
upon the astounding order of nature and human nature
that enhances both without violating either, and real
science that is intensely immersed in the beautiful riot of
living things rather than staring at microscopes, computer
screens, and the cold abstraction of formulas and models.

Conclusion

I realize, in coming to the close of this book, that I have only skimmed the surface of what could be said about a truly catholic ecology, an understanding of nature and human nature that could help to heal the cultural divide between the Left and the Right in regard to the environment by bringing their respective half-truths into a whole synthesis. But it is a beginning that can, at least, turn fruitless squabble into a fruitful debate and advance.

If each side can now see, as the other side has long seen so clearly, that the promethean violation of natural limits is destructive, and that environmental pollution and moral pollution are equally heinous, then we will have made significant headway.

What both sides need to understand is how delicate nature and human nature are, and how little we human beings know of the deep complexity of each. Unfortunately, following the Baconian paradigm we have feverishly sought with equal passion ever-increasing technological power, but we have not sought the wisdom to use it well. That wisdom comes, in great part, from nature itself, from a profound, sustained contemplation of its order, in all its levels, in all its particularities. Because we know that small changes can have devastating consequences, we need to look a lot more deeply before technologically leaping.

But if such small human-made changes can have such large, unanticipated devastating effects in nature, then the Left should be shaken awake by the real possibility that the same can be true of human nature. Can human beings, as a species, withstand continual radical social experiments with what constitutes marriage, what constitutes the family, what constitutes gender, what constitutes a moral life, and expect that human nature itself won't suffer ill effects as drastic as those predicted to effect nature by global warming enthusiasts? How can hedonism be bad for the environment but good for human nature? Is the Left willing to look at the facts in regard to human nature as carefully and thoroughly as it demands that the Right should in regard to global warming?

A truly catholic ecology looks at both sides, and takes both sides seriously, environmental ecology and moral ecology in one grand vision. The way we treat nature and the way we treat human nature go hand in hand, because they really are connected. When the Right treats the environment as a disposable resource to be consumed and cast aside at its whim, then it shouldn't wonder if the Left treats human beings as a disposable resource that can be endlessly, eugenically manipulated and disposed of through abortion and euthanasia. And vice versa. But a new respect for nature by the Right and human nature by the Left would have a deep, healing effect, creating a culture than affirms and protects both. If I may quote the pope again, at some length, since he says it better than I can,

> The way humanity treats the environment influences the way it treats itself, and vice versa. This invites contemporary society to a serious review of its life-style, which, in many parts of the world, is

prone to hedonism and consumerism, regardless
of their harmful consequences. What is needed
is an effective shift in mentality which can lead
to the adoption of *new life-styles* "in which the
quest for truth, beauty, goodness and communion
with others for the sake of common growth are
the factors which determine consumer choices,
savings and investments." Every violation of soli-
darity and civic friendship harms the environment,
just as environmental deterioration in turn upsets
relations in society. . . .

*The Church has a responsibility towards crea-
tion* and she must assert this responsibility in the
public sphere. In so doing, she must defend not
only earth, water and air as gifts of creation that
belong to everyone. She must above all protect
mankind from self-destruction. There is need for
what might be called a human ecology, correct-
ly understood. The deterioration of nature is in
fact closely connected to the culture that shapes
human coexistence: *when "human ecology" is respected within society, environmental ecology also benefits.*
Just as human virtues are interrelated, such that
the weakening of one places others at risk, so the
ecological system is based on respect for a plan
that affects both the health of society and its good
relationship with nature.

In order to protect nature, it is not enough
to intervene with economic incentives or deter-
rents; not even an apposite education is sufficient.
These are important steps, but *the decisive issue is
the overall moral tenor of society.* If there is a lack
of respect for the right to life and to a natural

death, if human conception, gestation and birth are made artificial, if human embryos are sacrificed to research, the conscience of society ends up losing the concept of human ecology and, along with it, that of environmental ecology. It is contradictory to insist that future generations respect the natural environment when our educational systems and laws do not help them to respect themselves. The book of nature is one and indivisible: it takes in not only the environment but also life, sexuality, marriage, the family, social relations: in a word, integral human development. Our duties towards the environment are linked to our duties towards the human person, considered in himself and in relation to others. It would be wrong to uphold one set of duties while trampling on the other. Herein lies a grave contradiction in our mentality and practice today: one which demeans the person, disrupts the environment and damages society.[1]

You perhaps think that I'm quoting Pope Francis again, from his encyclical *Laudato si'*. But these are actually the words of Pope Benedict XVI, from his encyclical *Caritas in veritate* ("Charity in Truth"). The former Cardinal Ratzinger—who before being elevated to the papacy was called "the pope's Rottweiler" by some who did not like him holding fast to the Church's moral teaching—strongly upheld *both* the necessity of ecology and moral ecology, the respect and care for nature and human nature. That is

---

[1]   Pope Benedict XVI, Encyclical Letter on Integral Human Development in Charity and Truth *Caritas in veritate* (June 9, 2009), §51.

the fullness of catholic ecology, which is, of course, also Catholic ecology, with a big "C."

Perhaps Pope Benedict's words may act as a sufficient incentive for both the Left and the Right to look more deeply into Catholic ecology, with a big "C." There is indeed a great treasure house of wisdom in the Catholic Church which has, for nearly two millennia now, been contemplating and explicating both catholic and Catholic ecology. Contrary to what many think on both the Left and Right, a truly catholic ecology is fully supported by—and I should add transformed by—Catholic ecology.

In order to get the cultural conversation started, I aimed at explicating the little "c" in this book, but another very wonderful book could be written built upon this natural and universal foundation, showing how Catholic doctrine both protects and glorifies nature and human nature. Actually, many books have already been written, if one cared to start searching through the great treasure house.